Shaping the Future of Your Business

Heino Hilbig

Shaping the Future of Your Business

How To Enable Your Organisation To Manage Market Changes and Crises

Springer

Heino Hilbig
Mayflower Concepts
Hamburg, Germany

ISBN 978-3-658-35348-3 ISBN 978-3-658-35349-0 (eBook)
https://doi.org/10.1007/978-3-658-35349-0

This Springer imprint is published by the registered company Springer Fachmedien Wiesbaden GmbH part of Springer Nature.
The registered company address is: Abraham-Lincoln-Str. 46, 65189 Wiesbaden, Germany

Foreword

The Day After Corona: Thoughts on the Second Edition

When I started planning the second edition of this book, corona was only mentioned as something going on in a province in China. The changes I had planned for the new edition were almost exclusively updates. Because the world is turning so fast, examples in a book about the future from 3 years before already seemed outdated. For example, the then VW board member Müller considered "autonomous driving to be a hype that could not be justified by anything" (Spiegel Online 2015). Meanwhile, Matthias Horx, who describes himself as a futurologist, declared with conviction that autonomous vehicles would be ready for the market in 20 years at the earliest (Bauer 2016). I am sure that both of them are already regretting these statements today.

Today, in July 2021, as I write this foreword, mankind is still in the middle of the first, second, or even third wave of the corona pandemic. We see a global human tragedy of immeasurable proportions. As of today, no one knows how bad the situation will become. I included. Although I professionally deal with future scenarios and appropriate corporate strategies, I am very reluctant to make predictions—as you will learn later in this book—for good reason. By the time this book is published, we will have hopefully overcome the worst of it—at least in Western Europe. Unless we are caught in another wave or mutant, the virus will then be a part of history, with companies back in business and the economy moving steeply upward again. And as for today? Is it back to business as usual?

It should not be. Hopefully, one thing will have thoroughly changed: company owners, managing directors, and managers should have learned from this crisis that it is not possible to run a company and creating long-term strategies without giving sound thought to future developments. And hopefully, they will consider the negative, through a well-developed crisis management system, as well as the positive, which is managing long-term strategies.

At this moment—in the middle of the pandemic—one must get the impression that, despite past assertions to the contrary, none of this has been established in companies. Lobbyists and industry experts are receiving a lot of public attention by claiming that their respective industry has suffered particularly from the economic consequences of the virus. Global corporations such as Boeing (Tageschau.de 2020) and the major airlines have put themselves under state supervision (Otley 2020).

What has yet to be reported—as of June 2021—is how many companies have already dealt with crisis scenarios and have therefore been able to pull one finished plan or another out of the bag. Why not? Could it be that hardly any medium-sized company has prepared itself for a crisis of this magnitude?

A typical argument in defense is that you cannot prepare for something like this.

Wrong! Of Course, You Can! Maybe you cannot prepare for the world coming to a standstill. But your company failing completely due to adverse circumstances over an indefinite time is unpleasant, although, unfortunately, a realistic scenario for several thousand companies every year: There are no accurate figures on this, but it is presumed that in Germany alone, 100,000 house searches by police are carried out every year. How many does that mean in Europe or worldwide? During which the central computing system is often seized as evidence. Please ask yourself: How active could your company remain if your computing system were to be unplugged at 6 a.m. tomorrow?

Can you prepare for it? No, you must! This book does not deal with the corona crisis specifically. It deals much more with planning options, identifying possible future conditions at an early stage, and how to integrate them into corporate strategies. This could be drastic changes in your market, new technologies, new competitors, or game-changing moves in society.

The tools that I present to you in Chap. 5 of this book are ideally suited to this future planning. The scenario technique (Sect. 5.3) and the business wargame (Sect. 5.4) can be used for effective crisis management as well.

For the "post-virus era," I would like to particularly recommend that you, a decision-maker within your company, pay attention to treacherous thoughts such as "this only happens every 100 years." Only when you successfully avoid such thoughts and discard the apparent certainty about what will happen, and only when you start to look for permanent coming changes, will you be able to optimally prepare your company for the future. Stay curious and questioning!

I wish you, your employees, and your relatives good luck and health for the coming months (from today's perspective) and hope that you will seize the opportunity arising from this crisis: Prepare your company for a change. Now would be the right time for it!

Mayflower Concepts
Hamburg, Germany

Heino Hilbig

References

Bauer W (2016) The end of 'I am my car'. https://www.automotive.at/kfz-wirtschaft/das-ende-von-ich-bin-mein-auto-124019 Accessed 11 May 2020.

Otley T (2020) These airlines have received a bailout. https://www.Businesstraveller.com/features/these-airlines-have-received-a-bailout/. Accessed: 11 May 2020

Spiegel Online (2015) Porsche boss calls self-driving cars 'hype'. http://www.spiegel.de/auto/aktuell/porsche-chef-matthias-mueller-bezeichnet-autonomes-fahren-als-hype-a-1,052,688.html. Accessed: May 18, 2020

Tageschau.de (2020) Boing calls for government aid. https://www.tagesschau.de/wirtschaft/boeing-251.html. Accessed: May 11, 2020

Foreword

Our company exists because another made a mistake and misjudged its future. You could sum up the history of Microplex Printware AG as simply as that. Of course, it is not quite that simple, but there is a grain of truth in this sentence: When our founder launched the company in 1987, most members of our team were highly qualified employees of Olympia Büromaschinen AG, which was dissolved four years later. We were pursuing a technology whose value had been underestimated at Olympia.

For us, dealing with future developments is not only technologically indispensable, but it has also somehow been ingrained in us.

Unlike Olympia, however, we are not a corporate group, but rather a medium-sized company with international operations. If we tried to establish classic innovation management developed for large companies, it would overtax our resources. We have neither the employees nor the time to implement such elaborate structures.

But should medium-sized companies, therefore, limit their success exclusively to the current four P's and leave dealing with the future to chance? Or should you rely on the fact that your employees and managers will come up with something in a time when the future is just around the corner? Waiting and seeing, that is quite clear, is not a solution.

Just as the way a medium-sized company deals with marketing and sales or production follows its own rules, certain principles must also apply when dealing with the future. For this, you need methods that take into account the decision-making processes of a medium-sized company just as much as they are pragmatic—methods that aim for clean success instead of mumbo jumbo that promises the big hit, the visionary product, or the revolutionary business model.

Because one should not be mistaken about this: The perhaps 100 German companies that manage to make such a big splash for the future each year stand in contrast to over 3.5 million companies that do not make the headlines, 75,000 of which are medium-sized companies alone.

Nevertheless, even without spectacular product innovations, companies can and must embrace the changes that future markets and technologies will require. The often demonized digitalization or globalization, for example, is both a curse and an opportunity. The decision whether to give the thumbs up or thumbs down depends solely on the attitude of the management and the preparation of the company.

For this preparation, this guidebook offers both a lot of introductory information that summarizes the most important basics of future planning in an easy-to-read form and concrete suggestions for implementation in the company. The whole thing is supplemented by many case studies, which can be used to study winning and losing strategies. Once you have decided to take concrete action, you are sure to find the right path for your own company after reading this book.

And since *Shaping the Future of Your Business* also manages the balancing act between serious information and an entertaining style of writing, I hope you, the reader, enjoy reading it.

Chairmen of the Board
Microplex Printware AG
Varel, Germany
November 2017

Olaf Mergili

Contents

About the Author

Heino Hilbig born in 1958, has worked as a marketing director for well-known brands such as Casio, Time/system, and Olympus, since 1985. The products of these companies let technological changes, innovation management, and long-term strategic orientation be a constant focus of his work.In 2011, he founded the management consultancy *Mayflower Concepts* in Hamburg, which is primarily concerned with growth and innovation concepts. He is also a frequently booked keynote speaker on future topics.Other works by Heino Hilbig published by Springer Gabler:***Marketing ist eine Wissenschaft … und die Erde eine Scheibe (2013):*** *(Marketing is a science … and the earth is a disc (2013)):* An amusing system critique about the small and big mistakes of marketing.)***Marketing sucht Zielgruppe … oder: Was macht der Gorilla am POS? (2015)****: (Marketing seeks for target groups … or: What is the gorilla doing at the POS? (2015)):* A scientific yet entertaining treatise on the things that are usually taboo among marketers.

List of Figures

1 About the Inability to Predict the Future

Abstract

Nothing seems to be more persistent in companies than the belief that managers can, at least roughly, predict the future of their own market. Particularly long and successful industry affiliation appears to be one of the factors that support this conviction. This first chapter shows how unspeakably wrong one can be about this, why it is impossible to predict the future with human abilities and why Excel-based number crunching has nothing to do with the future.

I confess, after my company was founded, I was busy for a while thinking about what catchy marketing description I could use for what we do: Together with our customers, we create future scenarios, develop strategies and implement measures with which these companies can prepare themselves for the future. Although this works well, it sounds too bulky to be suitable as a "speaking job title". So, I started looking for descriptions that could open the minds of potential customers and create a picture of what we do.

One of these terms was "futurologist"– a scientist and researcher in the field of future developments. If you enter this term in Google search, you will immediately receive a series of results and Google ads from people who are willing to offer their service as keynote speakers with future-oriented content for sometimes five-figure fees. There is nothing against that in itself. I, too, am giving keynote presentations on the future. It becomes difficult, however, when such "motivating keynotes" make statements about the future that cannot be justified by anything. A quite well-known German-speaking colleague, for example, made the statement in 2016 that we would not be driving in autonomous vehicles within the next 20 years—a state-

H. Hilbig, *Shaping the Future of Your Business*,
https://doi.org/10.1007/978-3-658-35349-0_1

ment that seems strange if you look at the autonomous systems that were already being tested all over the world, including in my hometown of Hamburg (Hamburger Hochbahn 2020, VW 2019). In 2020, the same colleague also took the view that there is no life on other planets (Poppe 2020). This surely is a field in which mathematicians, biologists, or physicists with a corresponding research focus may have a well-founded opinion. However, futurologists with a degree in sociology—like the colleague mentioned—probably do not have any information about this that would not be accessible to you or me. So, what exactly makes him a "researcher"?

"Futurologist"- could this be a profession that does not exist?

By definition, the future cannot be explored—it has not yet happened! That's why there are no lotto or roulette researchers either: Just for fun, try to find out the next number on a spinning roulette wheel—or the lotto numbers for the coming weekend. An odd request, right?

Now, one might object that these two games are purely random processes, whereas the future, that of your market for example, is by no means completely random, but is also determined by calculable factors such as technical or sociological developments. Unfortunately, this does not make the whole thing more predictable, but rather more complex. The iPhone, for example, was a product of the available technology and social acceptance by people. To put it plainly, the time was simply ripe for it. Now add an additional random factor: Just imagine, Steve Jobs fell madly in love with a Hawaiian princess a few years before the iPhone launch in 2007, with whom he lived happily for the rest of his life as a sugar cane farmer on a small island (for the more prosaic readers, perhaps as an alternative, he had a fatal car accident before 2007). Would there have been something like the iPhone anyway? And, if so, could this product have gone through the same triumphal procession?

The future cannot be explored nor can it be predicted. In any case, not much further than the next 3 years, as the US researcher Philip Tetlock has shown (we will go into his research results in more detail in Sect. 2.7). But what practical benefit do companies or congress organizers derive from futurologists who speak of flourishing landscapes or the end of the world in entertaining but also sometimes fact-free presentations?

From the very first edition of this book, my goal was to develop a methodical concept and to make it available in book form, which would allow assessment of future market developments and development of future strategies with a manageable amount of effort. Experience from many years of strategy development has shown me that it is not so much a matter of predicting future developments as precisely as possible, but rather of achieving a good balance between future assessment and strategic action. That is why I have deliberately refrained in my business life as well as in this book from relying on digital simulations and the like. On the one hand, after decades of corporate planning, I am deeply convinced that such simulations will ultimately only deliver a misleading result with dangerously false precision, no less. On the other hand, with the concept presented here, which is not bound to Excel-based figures, future management can be implemented for medium-sized companies with manageable resources, even without expensive simulation software.

In this edition of the book, I was able to reduce some complexity by taking out some elements and methods that have proven to be not necessary for practice, such as "Google Day". The future process is thus more stringent and hopefully easier to implement as an internal workshop. However, since such methods can have value in the everyday life of a company, for example, when it comes to initiating creative processes, I kept those tools available in a separate new Chap. 5 "Toolbox for the future". Creating future strategies is neither witchcraft nor the extremely secret insider knowledge of a few futurologists, but real, down-to-earth strategy work. You can find all the information you need in the daily press and on the Internet. And you will find all the methodology you need here. I promise you that!

1.1 A Future Concept Especially Medium-Sized Companies?

Since the dramatic times of the "unsinkable" Titanic, at the latest, we have known that large ocean liners are not very flexible. While they are highly efficient when it comes to performance figures such as costs per passenger per kilometer travelled, they only have little chance of success in the event of sudden course changes. And yes, they tend to overestimate their importance and their own power when it comes to the size of passing icebergs.

Those who attach more importance to flexible units that can also sail around an unexpected iceberg at short notice and with an eye to the future are more likely to choose smaller ships, but pay for this with significantly more discomfort—especially on heavy seas.

Both types of ships not only have very specific characteristics but also function differently as business units. To successfully steer huge enterprises (the corporate brothers and sisters of Titanic), a large number of highly specialized functionaries are required, who work together according to precisely defined work plans and, with equally detailed communication plans, ensure that the right decisions can be made at the right time. The case is completely different with small or medium boats. There, the engineer is also the first machinist, the second helmsman and possibly, the cook.

For me, there is hardly a better comparison to illustrate the difference between international groups on the one hand and medium-sized companies on the other. Both systems obviously work splendidly, but in completely different ways—which, by the way, is one of the reasons why the rise of a medium-sized company to the status of a corporate group is rarely successful and if it is, it is often a very painful process.

Any medium-sized company that tries to use methods that were conceived for enterprises runs the risk of merciless failure. This is especially true when it comes to future management. Whereas corporations can drive over icebergs with their own mass (which doesn't always work!) or get involved in strategic future planning at an early stage because of the large number of employees and sophisticated organisational forms, a typical medium-sized company needs other methods that are less personnel-intensive and resource-consuming. However, the main reason for a lack of future management in medium-sized companies often lies somewhere else, because there is a really massive obstacle that must first be overcome: The usually enormous knowledge (attention, please read correctly: Knowledge—not ignorance!) of the entrepreneur, managing director or decision-maker about the industry and market. This may sound contradictory, but on closer inspection, it can easily be explained. Sometimes, these managers have made every effort over many stages of their careers to become specialists in their market and to be able to understand every move a customer makes or to qualitatively classify every launch of a competitive product. If despite all these experts on board, consultants show up asking whether this perfectly positioned company is well prepared for the future, there can only be one answer to that question: "Yes, of course, if not us, then who?" After all, they have prepared themselves over years for what is usually fierce competition in the respective industry, have fought their way through and may nowadays even play a leading role in their own market. And then this consultant comes along and asks this seemingly absurd question.

Now, the consulting industry does indeed have, not entirely wrongly, at best a limited positive image to companies—I may say that, because I have played on both sides. When it comes to the future, however, a consultant has an unbeatable advantage over any internal manager: they view a market and the activities in it from the outside and the internal structures from a higher perspective, something like a qualitative helicopter. What you get to see from up there are often industries that have developed a modus operandi over decades and have formed an almost conspiratorial community of insiders. Manufacturers, distributors and retailers have such strict rules on how to deal with new products, marketing budgets and customer service that outsiders usually find it rather difficult to get into this business.

Please check how many top positions in your industry have been awarded to industry insiders recently. Many? Almost all? This could be a clue! And so, the question arises whether entrepreneurs, managing directors, board members, and division/department heads, with their specialist knowledge, are well prepared for market changes. In fact, companies in a particular sector are hardly able to set the impetuses they need to radically renew themselves when a radical change is imminent. If you look at the history of great innovations, it is often the already mentioned outsiders—companies from outside the industry—who set these incentives.

This was already going on in the Bible, when a hobby handyman built a ship to save life, while the otherwise responsible industry insiders still relied on praying. It went on with the renewal of the transport system, which was taken up by an engineer (instead of the horse breeders responsible up to that point), and unfortunately it continues in the present day. Just think of

- the renewal of the music business, which was carried out by a computer company (Apple) instead of the music industry
- the breakthrough of digital photography, which was achieved by a product from an electronics supplier (Casio) instead of the traditional camera manufacturers
- the radical change in the soft drinks market (introduction of energy drinks) by a hitherto unknown company from Austria (Red Bull) instead of the then most expensive company in the world (Coca-Cola)
- the complete upheaval in the German clothing market (online instead of offline) by the start-up company Zalando
- the up-to-now-leader in the e-mobility market is an absolute outsider from the car market (Tesla)

to name but a few.

Such innovators have not always been able to profit from their innovation in the long term or sustainably. And traditional companies have not always looked clumsy in the long run. The automotive industry, for example, currently seems to be winning back the market just in time. Whether Tesla will play a role outside the niche in the long term is highly uncertain. Even the camera manufacturers took up this fight starting in 1996, and with a delay of 2 years, were able to win—Casio stopped offering cameras after a few years.

However, this last example in particular shows that even with such an experience, it does not mean that companies are better prepared for the future: A good 10 years later, there was another side attack on classical photography—this time from the cavalry of smartphone manufacturers, which once again caught the traditional photo industry completely unprepared. Today, this industry produces an annual nine million cameras worldwide, compared to the over 120 million cameras in 2011 (CIPA 2020). The trend is steeply falling, even without the influence of the coronavirus. This once highly emotional market has now degenerated into a nostalgic microniche.

But how is it that an experienced, market-dominating company like Coca-Cola failed with its introduction of the energy drink KMX in the early 2000s, while an unknown, (then) regional and medium-sized company like Red Bull was stirring up the global soft drink market? Or: how is it possible that all the major music labels, with all their experience in dealing with musicians and fans, did not foresee—nor prepare for—the changes in the music market, while a nearly bankrupt, small computer company (Apple) and its spleeny interim CEO (Steve Jobs) made this very change by introducing the iPod and iTunes?

The answer is as simple as it is frightening: managers (and thus their companies) underestimate the willingness to change in their own market and overestimate their own ability to take a helicopter perspective. This is not meant to be pejorative in any way. Each of the managers that I spoke with in the past had acquired so much knowledge and experience over many years, that they were able to become successful.

In fact, several scientifically explainable influences limit a person's ability to perceive the world with a critical lens and, consequently, to prepare for the future. We will deal with this more intensively.

Anyone aware of these influences should be able to avoid mistakes that some of the very big brands have made and others have avoided very well. Examples from the nearly endless catalogue of bankruptcies and winners can then be found in Chap. 3.

Although this book is mainly aimed at managers of medium-sized businesses, I have used examples of content, methods and stories that were conceived for or have happened in corporate groups. This has to do with the fact that I also want to entertain you on your journey into the future and case studies of well-known brands can simply be packed into interesting stories more easily and with less explanation than success stories of hardly known companies. But you can be assured that there are both sad and really good examples from mid-sized companies as well. I've sprinkled a few of these in from time to time. You will find, as well, methods created for large enterprises, such as the scenario technique invented by Shell. We simply adapted them to the possibilities and needs of medium-sized companies. And so, by this, they became more useful for companies of all sizes.

1.2 Preparing for the Future Requires above all Else

Actually, creating a strategy is not rocket science. If you want to prepare your company for the future, you have to think about what that future will look like and then make the right plans for it. Unfortunately, this is easier said than done, because the beginning requires a mental journey into a world that is similar to ours, but which nobody can really imagine—nor has any of our ancestors ever have been able to imagine.

Please try to put yourself in the shoes of the generation in the middle of the last century—say around 1955. How did they imagine their future—let's say the year 2022? On the one hand, there were the gloomy Big Brother scenarios that George Orwell came up with in the aftermath of the Third Reich, but on the other hand, there was the beautiful technology that Captain James T. Kirk was able to use on his starship, the USS Enterprise. How far away the imagination of the generation of that time was from reality can be seen in an analysis by some US scientists who in the 1970s examined the technologies of the first season of the TV series Star Trek (recorded in the late 60s) in terms of their possibility of being realised. Regarding Captain Kirk's mobile communication device, they concluded that making calls from anywhere around the globe would be quite feasible, but 50 years later at the earliest. Let's look forward to it… the invention of the mobile phone must now be imminent!

We are having a good laugh now. But did any of us really foresee just a few years ago that the EU would become smaller instead of larger? Did anyone suspect that some people would do without milk for animal welfare reasons and become a massive target group for marketers? Was it conceivable that we would turn the light on at home by talking to a small black box from a bookseller (Amazon Alexa)? For the generation 50 years ago, all this would have sounded like science fiction!

The biggest problem in timely strategy preparation is our imagination. More precisely, our sometimes insufficiently developed imagination. So, at the beginning of a workshop or lecture, I usually tell a story about the future. A story about autonomous electric cars that can be called on-demand, resulting in quiet, green city centres; clothes that come from 3D printers; mobile systems that use speech to tell whether someone is telling the truth or (consciously) lying; restaurants that serve steaks purely created in a laboratory without any animal suffering; and lastly about people who will have a normal life expectancy of 100 years or more.

I then let my audience make guesses how far in the future this story will play out. Mostly, I am given periods of 30 to maximum 50 years. A period of time that is clearly too long, considering the developments have already been realized. Let's take a look:

The Electrically Powered Automobile

The critical success factors of this technology are battery range, charging infrastructure and cost.

- Already today, a battery charge at Tesla can cover 600 km under favourable conditions. In March 2020, Samsung presented the prototype of a new solid-state battery (Samsung 2020), which will not only be smaller and lighter than previous car batteries but will also be able to drive 800 km on one battery charge and tolerate 1000 charging cycles. Electric cars would then go further than cars today with combustion engines.
- In 2017, there were 6000 charging points in Germany and 16,000 petrol stations. In 2020, the ratio is already 19,500 charging points to 14,500 filling stations (Statista 2020).
- Building an electric car is technically far less demanding than building a car with a combustion engine, where you have to construct an 8-cylinder engine from a total of 1200 parts. When an electric motor is assembled, only seventeen parts are put together (Focus Online 2016). Since building an electric vehicle is definitely easier, there are far more start-ups dealing with this topic than there have been newcomers to the technology of vehicles with combustion engines. Just think of the German company StreetScooter GmbH, which was able to offer and build market-ready vehicles for the international parcel service DHL. And, this design advantage of e-mobility means that electric vehicles are expected to be available at lower prices than vehicles with combustion engines from 2025 onwards.
- This changeover is further accelerated by initial actions. The louder the voices of those who see the future of the automobile differently from today's construction became, the more traditional manufacturers started working on some form of electric mobility. And with every new voice, the pressure grew on those left behind to finally become active themselves. As a result, practically every traditional car manufacturer today is building e-vehicles.
- As soon as the changeover begins in the major industrialised countries, the changing infrastructure suddenly becomes the biggest supportive argument. Due to declining demand, conventional petrol stations or car workshops will increasingly convert or even close down in a few years. These thinned-out supply networks then will influence the decision of consumers making new purchases. And so on.

From 2025, the changeover from the combustion engine to the electric car could thus be drastically accelerated.

Vehicles Will Be Autonomously Driving

The last DARPA Urban Challenge (DARPA 2007) took place more than 10 years ago, in 2007. This was a competition announced by the US Department of Defense in which autonomous cars had to master a nearly 100-km long trip with a wide variety of traffic and road situations, including inner-city ones, completely on their own. Of the 55 cars registered, eleven reached the semi-finals and most of them crossed the finish line safely. This proved that this technology, although it did not yet look pretty, was basically ready for use—mission accomplished.

On June 23, 2017, Germany was one of the first countries in the world to enact a law that regulates the use of autonomous vehicles—still very cautiously—with the amendment of the Road Traffic Act (Bundesministerium der Justiz und für Verbraucherschutz 2017). However, because the legislators were aware that this technology would develop at breakneck speed, the law included an obligation to review the regulations every 10 years. And finally, in May 2021, the German government modified this law again, allowing Level 4 autonomous vehicles to participate in regular road traffic from 2022.

Almost every new vehicle today has the necessary components for autonomous driving: sensors that perceive the environment and control elements for acceleration, steering and brakes. How these tools are used today currently depends on the manufacturer. Some use these systems only as braking aids; others also use the control options as parking aids or distance-controlling cruise control. Tesla, the pioneer in the field of e-mobility, today allows its vehicles to be parked and unparked in the garage on their own if desired and, since 2016, has been delivering all models with hardware that is said to be sufficient for autonomy levels 4 and 5.[1]

Since April 2019, the VW Moia concept has been driving through the streets of my hometown, Hamburg, as a kind of shared taxi on demand. The 500 electric vehicles were designed by the VW Group as autonomous e-vehicles from the outset, even if they currently still need a driver. In May 2021, VW announced its intention to actually transport passengers autonomously with Hamburgs MOIA concept starting in 2025.

[1] Level 4: Full automation. The system permanently takes over the driving of the vehicle. If the driving tasks are no longer mastered by the system, the driver can be asked to take over. Highest level, level 5: No driver required. With the exception of setting the destination and starting the system, no human intervention is required.

At the same time, the same group is having a number of fully automated test vehicles cruise around Lake Alster in regular road traffic. Admittedly, this is just a field test with human drivers as backup. But hey, these cars are driving fully automatically in the thickest Hamburg rush hour traffic in the city center. And there has not yet been an accident reported.

As soon as the level of full driving automation (level 5) is reached, the main interest shifts from the question of "how cool the car can drive" (autonomous cars will not drive "cool"—they always drive in full compliance with all traffic regulations, safely and automatically—due to their programming!) to what you can do while driving. Depending on the purpose of the journey, a self-driving car could then be equipped inside as an office or with entertainment modules or even as a relaxation vehicle with sleeping facilities for long distances. Therefore, the trend could quite quickly move towards renting such cars—also attractive for their interior design—instead of buying your own vehicle, in the same way that you already call a large-capacity taxi today when you want to drive with more than four people. You don't buy one of those either, do you?

Future individual transport could therefore be a mixture of fully automated taxis and a car-sharing model—a thought that VW is currently exploring in a concrete project. From 2021, the market is to be made happy with autonomously driven car sharing (Stehle 2017).

This results in another advantage for the user: he no longer has to worry about battery charging times, because such car-sharing vehicles simply charge automatically when they are not booked by a customer. E-vehicles, therefore, do not necessarily require much greater battery capacity. The current battery-powered delivery vehicles at DHL, for example, cover a distance of just 80 km on one battery charge (up to 180 km for other companies) (DPD 2019) and require several hours of charging time. However, since these cars do not have to travel any further to deliver parcels in cities and since one night at a normal power outlet is enough to charge them, they are already fulfilling their purpose today. Quod erat demonstrandum.

As soon as autonomous driving becomes the norm, fewer accidents will occur due to increasing perfection. The head of VW Group Research predicts that the number of accidents will drop by up to 90% (Becker 2017). As a result, car insurance for manually driven vehicles will become more and more expensive. Also, legislators will first make "manual" driving significantly more expensive and later even make it almost impossible through corresponding restrictive regulations. Incidentally, there is a good reason for this: in the middle of a convoy of autonomous vehicles, which, for example on the motorway, travel one behind the other at a distance of only one meter without any traffic jam, a human-controlled vehicle would be a death trap.

The Inner Cities Become Quiet and Green

This step of my future scenario is a logical consequence of the previous one. Autonomous, networked cars need much less space to drive, because every vehicle can start and brake at the same time and thus drive much closer together—so-called "platooning". Where four-lane roads are needed in cities today, two lanes could suffice in the future for the same transport volume. If, in addition, there were hardly any private vehicles left standing around, parked for an average of 20 to 22 hours a day, we would probably have only 100 million cars in Europe today, or even fewer than that, instead of 290 million cars (2020). And instead of 500 million street parking spaces, we would only need 60 million. In such a situation, cities might start to demolish the roads in the inner cities. After all, a square meter of road that no longer exists no longer needs to be maintained and freed from potholes every year. Since the remaining vehicles—either battery-powered or hydrogen-powered—neither generate engine noise nor emit exhaust gases, the possibility of a green city is not so far away.

Tailor-Made Clothing from the 3D Printer

3D printers admittedly still sound like science fiction to many people. However, they already have an important commercial significance in all areas of research and the production of specialised, small series. The first commercially exploited shoes from the 3D printer have been available since 2014. In 2016, the American sprinter Allyson Felix became the first female athlete to run at the Olympic Games in Rio with 3D-printed shoes from Nike. Whether it was this occurrence that led Adidas to make all the other Olympic medal winners happy with 3D-printed shoes from Adidas is not known. But the company was certainly offering standard scanning and tailoring of sports shoes as early as 2015 (Adidas 2015).

Enjoy Meat without Killing Animals

This is one of the weaker parts of my vision of the future. Not because it is unlikely, but because there are different variants for this part, and not all of them do away with dead animals.

Firstly, there is the result of the Dutch scientist Mark Post, in-vitro researcher at the Physiological Institute of the University of Maastricht, who presented his first meat patty made from artificially produced meat as early as 2013 (Schalk 2016). All he needed were some pieces of the muscle meat of a cow. Well, the burger cost about 250,000 EUR and was probably only moderately tasty. But when I think back to my cooking beginnings, it was the same—just cheaper. So, let's give him a little more time to practice! Start-ups such as Mosa Meat (see Maastricht University

2017), Memphis Meats (Memphis Meats 2017) or SuperMeat (SuperMeat 2017) have, in any case, started to focus on the commercial aspect and hope to be able to produce such petri dish meat industrially from 2022 onwards and even offer it at a lower price than regular meat.

A German-based company called Rügenwalder Mühle is taking a completely different approach by producing meat-tasting, meat-looking and meat-feeling food from vegetarian raw materials. The burger and mortadella already meet these criteria in blind tests. Just imagine what can be achieved in the coming years when a medium-sized German company can get that far in just two and a half years of development time!

And then there's the variant that takes the most getting used to: even from insects, it is already possible to produce quite excellent meat substitutes—you just need to stop your imagination while eating!

Getting Old Healthy

The average life expectancy for men in Germany is just below, and for women just over, 80 years, with an upward trend. According to the Planck Institute for Demographic Research, girls born in Germany in 2019 can expect to live to an average age of 95 (Spiegel 2019). The prediction that we will achieve a life expectancy of over 100 years could therefore become reality before the end of this century.

The Truth App

As early as 2017, there was an app in both smartphone worlds that promised to be able to recognize feelings, based on 18 years of scientific research. Anyone who installed the *Moodies* app on his smartphone and talked to the app for 15 seconds was analyzed for his emotional status. Or should one rather say, dissected? After testing it myself, I can say that this app seems to work with acceptable reliability.

The next step will be optical recognition: the technique of recognizing microexpressions, that is, the tiny movements of our facial muscles that are supposed to tell everything about us if they can be read. Scientists are currently working on this as well.

Will these visions really come true exactly like this? To be honest, of course, I don't know. But the chance that these developments will radically change our lives is great. And probably even more radically than I have described. Let's take the example of the car. A lot of jobs will be lost (wanting to become a driving instructor will be a very stupid idea in times with autonomous cars), infrastructures will become obsolete (parking garages and private garages will become useless) and revenues that were thought to be secure will no longer flow (car insurance accounts for 40% of all insurance amounts). On the other hand, there will be many new developments (new profession: conversion specialist for old garages). If you want to go deeper into these topics, I recommend the really very logical-sounding essay by the American future speaker Thomas Frey (Frey 2017) or—very detailed with sources—the book *The Last Driver's License Holder Has Already Been Born* by Mario Herger (Herger 2018).

So almost every innovation that appears in my future history already exists today. But how long will it take for those ideas to turn into products that we will all use?

Let's try again. Please take a look at Fig. 1.1. When do you expect pictures like this to look completely different? Completely new constructions for vehicles—electric, autonomous, flying? Maybe significantly fewer units on the street. In short, how much time do you give the current car traffic concept before it is completely replaced by something else? Now, please make a guess. 30 years? Or even shorter—20? Couldn't be any shorter than that, could it?

Careful—I'll lead you back to the ice! In fact, there has already been such a massive turnaround in private transport. Figure 1.2 shows the so-called Easter

Fig. 1.1 When do you expect such a traffic situation to be changed? (Source: Adobe Stock, Mathieu Degrange, stock.adobe.com)

Fig. 1.2 Easter Sunday in New York 1900 (left) and 1913 (right). (Source: US Library of Congress (left), US National Archive (right))

Parade, an annual parade on Easter Sunday on fifth Avenue in New York. On the left, on April 15, 1900 with one exception, only horse-drawn carriages are in this parade. On the right, on March 23, 1913 they are—apart from one single horse—exclusively the ancestors of our cars today. It took just 13 years for a complete change in the transport infrastructure. What period did you type for the current traffic turnaround?

So, if you want to take a look into the future, you need a good dose of imagination. And above all, the freedom of thought to accept completely different options from those we know today. Why this step is (usually) very difficult for us, we will take a closer look at in Chap. 2.

▶ Please remember:
The path into the future usually starts with a question—but never with an answer!

1.3 Reality: Predictions without Imagination

If we want to talk about the preparation for the future and about the level of meaningful strategies, that is, how much money, time and manpower you should invest in such future scenarios, then the first thing you need is a significant amount of imagination. Unfortunately, when talking about the future, many people tend to look for "what will happen" rather than "what might happen" at first. Thus, their visions about the future almost look like concrete predictions. But what is the value of such predictions? Where are the limits and how do you recognise misjudgements—preferably before invest money into them?

If you look at management literature today that deals with preparing companies for the future, you will quickly find endless examples of the failure of big brands and dominant companies. And the longer that one looks at such examples, the more stunned authors seem to be at the fact that such large companies and powerful corporate leaders could have been so wrong.

- How could Charles Duell, the head of the US Patent Office, seriously believe in 1899 that "anything that can be invented" was already invented? And worse, how could he publicly state that?
- How could the most valuable and influential company in America at the time, the Western Union Telegraph Company, seriously refuse to buy Alexander Graham Bell's telephone patents in 1876?
- How could Daimler-Benz and its subsidiary AEG have misjudged in the early 1990s the newly awakening market for office communication (and abandoned their preparations for it)?
- And how could the Nokia board of directors simply block the issue of touch displays for its more complex mobile phones—which were not yet called smartphones at the time?

No question, all these misjudgments of past managers and influencers are easily recognizable as such, as long as one looks at these issues from the now—that is, practically with the knowledge of their future. And this is exactly the problem with such considerations, because we do not realise that we are in the same situation: What will our descendants in 2120 think about the decisions and assessments of our generation? Will they ask themselves why we actually bought vehicles that burn petroleum distillates when it was "already clear" that in a few years we would be driving electric cars and only paying for them when we use them? Or will they shake their heads because we have taken so much time to develop sensible health prevention in a highly networked world? Of course, our descendants could also question quite different things. I just don't know which ones, because I, like you, am part of this time and therefore not objective. I simply have no idea which self-evident things of the coming century I cannot imagine today and which imaginable ideas I completely misjudged. As Nobel Prize winner in economics Thomas Schelling once said, 'The one thing you cannot do, no matter how rigorous your analysis or heroic your imagination, is to make a list of things you never thought of' (Johnson 2018). Let's repeat that: you can't make a list of things you've never thought of.

What is exciting is that science fiction authors seem to have a better feel for such things in this respect. Just take a look on the web for inventions of the famous Star Trek series that have become real products (Zitt 2013): the mobile phone, the fax, the headset, the 3D printer—the list is long and growing steadily.

But this appearance is deceptive. In fact, today you can't describe anything that has yet to be invented, neither in a science fiction movie nor in a serious prognosis of the future. The second you describe it, you have already formulated the basic idea. Just imagine, tens of thousands of years ago, your and my ancestor sitting in a cave by the cosy fire and wondering when the wheel will finally be invented. The second the concept of a wheel was expressed, the essential part of the idea was born. The rest is craftsmanship—well, mostly anyway.

So, science fiction writers are no more reliable at predicting the future—they're just better at thinking up things you and I should have. And these ideas then inspire others to create such products. The Star Trek Communicator, which inspired Motorola and the former Siemens subsidiary Gigaset, is just one example. I first formulated this principle at lectures in the 1990s, when I was repeatedly asked what the cameras would look like in the future. That's why I was all the more pleased when I heard about the Phantastische Bibliothek Wetzlar, which is seriously engaged in analysing science fiction literature in order to compile ideas for future concepts on behalf of governments and corporations. What a nice idea (Phantastische Bibliothek Wetzlar 2020)!

So the future is still being baked. The beauty is: with every move you or your company do, you contribute to creating this future. Take, for example, the development of high-performance batteries. In the 1990s, the capacity of the rechargeable AA-type accumulators increased from approximately 600 mAh to more than 2700 mAh within a very short time. The runtime of a fully charged battery had been quadrupled without further ado. Why so suddenly? After all, the potential for this technology had technically been around for a very long time. The answer is simple: digital cameras became popular and in the early years still needed a lot of power to heat the sensor and to supply the first LCD displays with energy. The first generations of these cameras could take only 30 pictures with a set of normal alkaline batteries. Push the release button 30 times and then replace four expensive batteries? Even the previous film-based shooting felt more ecological! So as soon as the need for higher capacities was recognised, the technology became available.

Actually, this is a nice prospect for your future scenario. If you plan innovation, you are changing the future yourself. And that is why I fundamentally contradict ideas about waiting and seeing how things turn out. No matter how well you are positioned today, the cemetery of business is full of companies that wanted to wait and see what would happen.

1.4 Linear Thinking Prevents a Successful Future!

Please try to talk casually with colleagues about the future of your company—let's say over a period of 5 years from today. I bet you that for every idea of what might change in your market, you will find at least one colleague who doesn't believe in this change.

A Little Test

What do you think you'll use for phoning in five years? Well, most of you will undoubtedly believe that in five years, the smartphone will still be the defining heart of our communicative networking. Was I right? Most of the people with whom I did this test reacted in the same way.

But what if I told you that in the year 2022 the smartphone will be 15 years old already? What if I were stating that no technology has remained dominant for so long in these times? Take a look at the desktop PC. It only managed a paltry eleven years until it was pushed into a corner by laptops and notebooks. The classic mobile? Twelve years. The MP3 player? Ten years. And the smartphone is supposed to be the exception? A product that today, if we are honest, still looks exactly the same as it did when Steve Jobs first held it up on a stage during MacWorld in San Francisco, 2007? Although the cameras are better, the edges are rounded and the displays are bigger, that thing in your pocket is the spitting image of its grandfather.

At this point in your discussion with colleagues, there will usually be a long, reluctant "yeeeeeees … " (I've probably had this discussion a hundred times!): 'Yeeeees…, of course, the smartphone will be replaced at some point. But not in 5 years!'

If you now point to technological leaps, unfulfilled wishes for the performance of a communication device and the age of the smartphone in 2025, the conceded answer is 'yes, there is definitely something new—but I think most people will still be using their smartphone then.' You recognise the trap? (Fig. 1.3).

That's exactly how the colleagues on Kodak's board of directors acted in the 1990s because they simply couldn't imagine that digital photography would come that fast. You remember the Kodak brand, do you? Yellow logo, red lettering. That was the dominant company in the market, with hundreds of thousands of employees, an 80 percent market share of photographic paper and a similarly attractive share in the film.

Fig. 1.3 How are we going to phone tomorrow? (Source: Adobe Stock, HiQuality, stock.adobe.com)

Or the colleagues in the offices of the already quoted Western Union Telegraph Company, who simply could not imagine that news could be transmitted across the continent other than by tapping in code. The president of the society, William Orton, in his rejection of Bell actually spoke of "toys without commercial value"! (Santoso 2008).

All of us (and no, I am not excluding myself from this consideration) have a very strong urge that we do not want to see the circumstances of our life and work changed in any way. We believe that the next 5 years will actually be just like the last five. An effect which—just as unsurprisingly—somehow only ever continues. Looking back, the change from the elegant mini mobile phone to the smartphone is of course completely (!) logical for all of us. But if in 2006—one year before the presentation of the iPhone—someone had asked whether one could imagine that 5 years later the vast majority of people would be making phone calls with practically a PC in their pocket—hardly bigger than a sandwich toothpick—one would have laughed at the poor man. After all, who would have wanted to swap the super-small folding phone for such a brick back then?

And there have been many such "completely impossible" views in recent history. If you had told someone in the 1960s that today you turn the lights on and off at home with your phone, put little aluminium capsules in a vending machine and then drink a perfectly staged cappuccino, and travel in some countries on trains that go faster than airplanes could fly back then, they would have taken you for a complete science-fiction freak.

But the people at that time were by no means fools or stupid. They had all the skills that we have today. They were just not as well versed in the technical and social development of the third millennium as we are today. They have not been able to imagine the future halfway right, just as all the generations before them have not been able to do so. We know that this is the case, yet it does not seem possible for us to learn from this situation and look at the future as openly as we look at the past. On the contrary, we scale our present linearly up and keep it for the future.

Of course, it is conceivable that we will have faster mobile connections in the future. But that shortly, in 5 years, we will be able to access any volume of data anywhere in the world and without waiting, so that our smartphone successor will be able to do things that only large server farms can today, cannot be possible?

Yes, in a few years we will be sitting in cars with electric drive and sophisticated self-driving functions. But the fact that at the end of the next decade we may hardly have any private individual transport at all, but will call an "e-mobile" when we need it, simply cannot be? Absolutely out of the question?

Such a limitation of thoughts is the consequence of the upscaling and extrapolation of the present and happens with us humans practically automatically. It is essential to know the reasons for this before you start to think about the future of your own company or industry. Only if you know these traps in advance and always keep an eye on them will you have a chance in developing future scenarios that are somehow close to what is really coming.

Under no circumstances, however, should you believe that the future—even after only 5 years—will look something like our present. Anyone who simply assumes the future to be a linear extension of the past and present could make a fatal mistake for their company.

1.5 Those Who Do Not Prepare Lose out: Even in the Age of Pandemics

Please, just name a few companies that you felt have always existed.... Thanks! That seem to have been easy. What about big companies that always should have been there, of which perhaps is still a brand left that is now used by some, mostly Asian, company? More difficult? How about the once-famous German mail-order company QUELLE Versand, American Online (AOL), Time/system, Grundig, CompuServe, Schlecker, Dual? An ultimate Internet provider; one of the largest, even internationally, active mail-order company; and a market-dominating drugstore chain: competitors, customers, dealers, employees—all stakeholders at that time would have sworn stone on stone that these companies would always remain in the market. And then something came up and oops—everything was different. An event comes completely unpredictably and has a massive impact on an industry, a market or even an entire society. In the case of these companies, the "short-term capital requirement" (Schlecker) or the "technology change" (AOL) has hit hard and relentlessly.

Honestly, do you believe that your company or your industry is completely "safe"? That your employer will still exist 20 years from now? Just think, these virus-driven days, of the German airline Lufthansa, the aircraft builders Airbus and Boeing or any other huge, traditional enterprise. Everyone thinks that their own business is indestructible, will be the *Keiunkan*[2] of their industry. But is this really the case? Do you believe that your company will still exist in two decades?

In the early 1990s, US scientist Jim Collins and his team analysed historical data on hundreds of American companies to unravel the secret of success. To do this, he took the turnover curves of companies that had been around for a long time, divided them into those that had grown in line with the market and those with outstanding growth, and then compared the history, actions and people involved in both groups. The culture and working methods of the hyper-successful companies should actually have guaranteed a bright future for those companies, or so the theory goes. It will probably come as no surprise to you that some of these extraordinarily successful companies have nevertheless managed to slip into mediocrity. The reasons for this were different at IBM than at Philip Morris or American Express, but many of the superstar companies of that time are only mediocre today and may not even exist in another ten or 20 years.

Thomas J. Peters and Robert H. Waterman (1986) examined 62 companies that had excelled in their book *In Search of Excellence*. It was the same outcome: half of these once outstanding companies have now been bought up, merged with other companies or simply gone bankrupt.

And, to complete the list, in his work *The Halo-Effect*, Philip M. Rosenzweig (2014) describes how out of the 500 companies on Standard & Poor's 1957 top list, four decades later, so in 1997, no fewer than 74 are still on the Top 500 list. Some of the others have merged with other companies, but most have either shrunk below the valuation threshold or are populating the great graveyard of sad companies.

Why do we believe that this could not happen in the present? Why does hardly anyone think it possible that Google, Facebook or Amazon, even, could be only moderately successful companies with a good chance of being taken over in 10 or 20 years? Why do we consider ourselves so much wiser than any generation before

[2] The Keiunkan is a hotel in Japan, and at 1300 years old, it is the oldest still in existence in the world. See: http://www.keiunkan.co.jp/en/.

us? Let's be honest, we know that even in 5 or 10 years' time we will look back and be just as amused about our simple-minded view of things today as we are about current hairstyles or eyewear fashion. Not only in the 70s was there weird thinking!

Surprising is that corporate leaders—whether managing owners, salaried board members or department heads—often seem to have little interest in the future. When asked whether they have prepared for possible changes in their market, I have received quite often a "you can't prepare for everything", sometimes combined with "when the time comes, we will react ".

Especially the current pandemic in 2020/21 makes it clear how highly dangerous this belief is. Because of the many entrepreneurs who did not manage to set the course in time, only the fewest can still be sought for questions. Their negligent handling of the future has usually not only cost them their own jobs, but many others as well, and sometimes even destroyed the entire company. I'm sure that the colleagues at Kodak would have given a lot back then for their management to act differently!

1.6 Try it yourself: Predict Just 24 Hours of your Life

So, we tend to view our future only as a linear continuation of the present. At the same time, governments, administrations, corporations and NGOs are investing billions of Dollar to predict the future. Why are we going after it so hard? Are such investments worthwhile? Can the future be predicted at all? Before we get into that, I would like to ask you to do a little self-experiment.

A Self-Experiment

Think about a normal day. A day in the future. The best thing to do is to take as boring a day as possible—one on which things in your life will follow a very fixed pattern. Tomorrow, for example. Or the day after tomorrow. Or next week Thursday, if that is a really predictable day.

Now take a pad, a pencil and start to predict and write down your day—let's say, since you are still a beginner as a prophet, a prediction for every quarter of an hour. So, for Thursday, with an average of 16 waking hours, you need about 64 such entries for your personal forecast. Mind you, this is not intended to be a plan that you will work through bit by bit on Thursday, but an assessment of what will actually happen.

Next Friday, you take this forecast and note—also every quarter of an hour—what has actually happened. Please do. I will wait for you here. I'll wait for you...

<….>

<….>

<….>

So, we are a few days further and you now have the result. It probably doesn't surprise you very much, does it? You were probably pretty far off with your forecasts, weren't you?

By the way, you are welcome to repeat this attempt. Scientific statistics require that you perform tests more frequently to ensure representative results. So, feel free to repeat the experiment as often as you like. The result will never be different.

Let's affirm that: even on the most boring day of your life, you—as the definitely biggest and by the way the only global expert on your own life—are not able to predict what will happen to you! Or to be a little more precise, you were not able to predict halfway precisely what would happen.

"Halfway precise" means, if you always let the alarm clock wake you up at half past six in the morning, you probably assumed that it would ring you awake at half past six on that day. That was probably the case, unless chance rushed by in the form of a power outage or the neighbour had to take a sick child away and was therefore already standing at your door at six o'clock. Or your life partner hit the alarm clock button yesterday and accidentally turned it off. You see, even with something as simple as a clock radio, there are plenty of imponderables.

And so it goes all day. If you were able to plan your daily routine on your own, you might have roughly sketched the day pretty well. But then you are probably not an executive, but a librarian of a monastery with a very, very quiet workplace in the fourth basement.

As soon as you have external contacts, it starts to become difficult. Suppose you are a librarian at the monastery in question, but you have an assistant. Then, you would also have to completely forecast his daily schedule to be able to predict when he could approach you with which topic and then calculate how this would change your day.

If you have not one but several encounters during the day (which should happen occasionally with managers), then you must not only correctly forecast each of the daily plans, but also the interactions that each of these people might have with others in turn. And then just imagine that you are not sitting in the basement of a monastery, but in the fully glazed open-plan office of an e-commerce provider. As you can see, it's getting very complex. So complex that it is not even possible to calculate the extent of the interactions and their effects.

If the idea of increasingly complicated interactions reminds you of billiards, you are not that wrong. For this game, the British physicist Sir Michael Berry already dealt with the question in an article published in 1978 on which influences one would have to know and calculate exactly in order to be able to predict not only the course of the first impact of billiard balls, but also all further movements after two, three, five or ten (theoretical) collisions. As early as the fifth or sixth shot, he came up with values in which the weight of spectators next to the table and their exact position played an essential, non-negligible role. From the 15th collision on, the position and the movement of each individual atom in the universe must be known and calculated in order to be able to predict the result with reasonable certainty, so the summary of his study goes (Berry 1978).

As you can see, there is a lot to come if you want to predict your future. It only gets better if you can do without precision. For example, if your forecast for the day is simply "Complete project A, have lunch with board member B and call customer C", then your forecast may be met to some extent (excluding coincidences and unplanned interactions). However, if you want to be more precise, the accuracy of your forecast becomes increasingly unlikely:

"I'll call customer C on Thursday" might still happen. "I will be on the phone with customer C on Thursday between 1 and 2 p.m." is already dependent on whether you and whether customer C are available at that time, feel like having a chat, with charged mobile phones and neither of you are on the phone with someone else. Furthermore, if you try to predict this phone call to the minute, you are unlikely to be successful—unless you want to win the small bet with me at all costs and are meticulously careful to make every minute-prediction happen by your own actions.

But then you yourself are interacting with your prediction (which is then actually no longer a prediction, but a plan) and would therefore even have to plan for the eternal comparison of the prediction with the current time. As you can see, the more accurately you want to predict the day, the more obstacles you face.

This complexity in dealing with future events is often represented by a structure that can be imagined as a kind of three-dimensional funnel, which is therefore also called the "future funnel"or "event funnel".

In Fig. 1.4, on the left is the starting point from which you want to start the future prediction. The further you wander to the right, the further you are in the future. The funnel now represents the number of possible events—and thus the multitude of possible futures—that could happen. From this funnel, two essential conclusions can now be drawn for your career as a prophet:

The further you move away from today, i.e. the present, the more diverse the possibilities of the future are. To put it more simply: for the next half hour you might be a good prophet, but for next Thursday you can only predict your life in broad outlines, and for the first Tuesday in October the year after next your predictions are really poor. And it is no different for me or any other future planner!

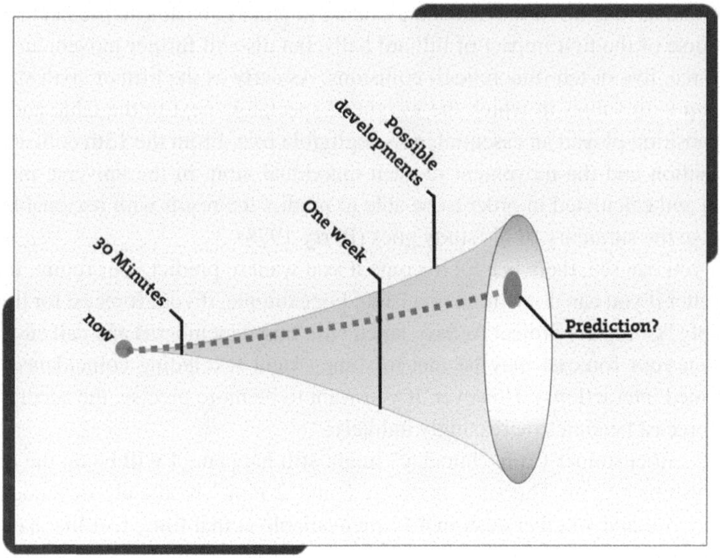

Fig. 1.4 The event funnel: The further the view into the future, the more possibilities of development there are and the more uncertain predictions become

The more precisely you can determine and delimit the area (the inner tube instead of the outer tube in Fig. 1.5) for which you want to make a forecast, the smaller the variability of the future will be. Or to put it more simply: if you only want to make predictions about your personal life, the corridor in which you have to look for the future will be smaller than if you want to predict the collective future of all the inhabitants of your city. That's why forecasts that are supposed to describe the future of humanity in 200 years are a real feat. But we'll get to that. I promise!

Before we do so, let's get back to your daily forecast for Thursday. It is now Friday, and we both agree that you—as the world's only one hundred percent expert on your life—did not manage to predict last Thursday even nearly accurately, right? What chance do prophets and other experts have of successfully addressing much larger issues? And what does this mean for your future management? Is it possible that you invested the money for this book in vain? Questions over questions—but ones we will address!

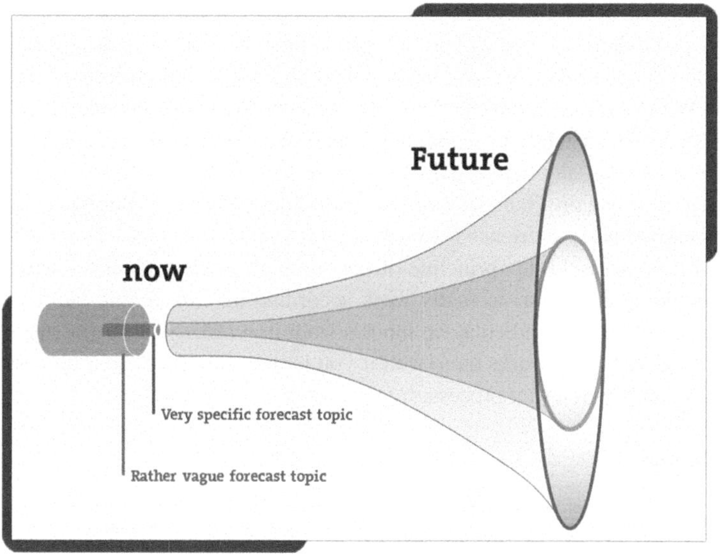

Fig. 1.5 The extended event funnel: The more diffuse the topic for which a prediction is to be made, the more uncertain forecasts become

1.7 What Can Big Data Really Do? And cannot?

Now, despite all the problems with the crystal ball discussed so far, there is a new soothsaying option that seems to be really promising for company managers. So promising that more and more authorities, governments and corporations are now spending millions of dollars to accumulate as much knowledge as possible—tremendous amounts of data—in order to predict how individuals will behave or societies will change. It seems like half of the strategy seminars today bear *Big Data* in the title. If you are about to invest in this topic, please read this section before you do so.

Big Data does not mean just the extensive collection of unimaginable amounts of data, but it includes the necessary hardware, the analysis tools and, last but not least, the analyst in front of the computer as well. The hope of many users—and the promise of some vendors—that you only have to fill hardware with endless amounts of data to get an answer in the style of DeepThought (the legendary computer in The Hitchhiker's Guide to the Galaxy) is unlikely to happen. Even DeepThought only managed to come up with a meagre "42" as an answer.

Let's go back to your self-experiment. To be able to solve the task of forecasting your next standard day, you will probably have thought about what usually happens on such a standard day. So, you have looked at the past and projected it into the future. With slight variations, perhaps, because you know that this month your assistant is driving his child to school in the morning and therefore will be arriving a quarter of an hour later than usual—or because the colleague with whom you usually have jour fixe on Thursdays will be on holiday next week. But basically, you simply carried past experience forward.

And it is precisely this principle of operation all mathematical forecast models—including Big Data—actually work according to: Concluding by observing the past and creating mathematical models from it in order to arrive at statements about the future. This works quite well if you look at single, singular processes or large, statistically relevant processes:

Example

Sir Isaac Newton is said to have been so traumatised by a falling apple that he established his theory of gravity. This states that an apple that detaches from a branch will land on the ground at a precisely predictable time. And for most of the apples in your garden, this prognosis is also correct.

In addition, you may also know from observations made in previous years that between August and November all the apples in your garden will go down this path, so you can make a corresponding forecast for this year. A statistically ascertainable process. The more you know about each individual apple—how it is suspended from the tree, what it weighs, what surface it will face, what degree of ripeness it is in, whether there is a strong wind—the more precisely you can narrow down when the apple will fall. That's the basic idea of Big Data.

But you still don't know that a single apple will actually reach the ground at the time calculated—after all, if it falls it could be artfully impaled by the beak of a passing black swan and carried away! ◄

There is no question: the more data a company has at its disposal, the better it can forecast the short-term future. If a certain customer group in an online shop has often looked at brown shoes after buying a green pair of trousers, this information should be used to keep interest in further purchases high. And if statistically hardly anyone puts the combination of bright red blouse and squeaky yellow trousers in the shopping basket, this combination can be excluded from the offer proposal. This is exactly how Amazon's "Customers who bought this also looked …" works.

Knowing as many details as possible is therefore the basic principle with Big Data. Physicists call this longing the Laplace demon. The French mathematician and physicist Pierre-Simon Laplace dreamt in the late eighteenth century (Dale and Laplace 1995, p. 2):

> An intelligence which, at a given instant, could comprehend all the forces by which nature is animated and the respected beings that make it up, if moreover it were vast enough to submit these data to analysis, would encompass in the same formula the movements of the greatest bodies of the universe and those of the lightest atoms. For such an intelligence nothing would be uncertain, and the future, like the past, would be open to its eyes.

Somewhat less poetically: if you could know exactly the location, status and movement of every part of the universe and put all this information together to form a complete picture, then you could describe the universe now and in the future.

Since a thing with computers was not quite so common in the eighteenth century, Laplace speaks of an "intelligence"—which led to the funny term of Laplace's demon. What Laplace describes here is nothing else but the (theoretical) ultimate goal for Big Data: The more detailed my information is, the better conclusions I can draw from it. If I know *all* the details, I can predict *everything*.

But the god of numbers and data has set three major hurdles before this ultimate result, which experts for big data warn of all over the world—if they are not employed by hardware and software manufacturers:

Hurdle 1: The Data Tsunami

Big Data needs data—an infinite amount of data—in order to turn it into information. "Data and information, isn't it the same thing?" you may now be thinking. It's not. In fact, there is a mile-wide difference! If I write down the sentence, 'Data is not information—it has to be interpreted', about 75,600 times, this results in a book of about 1500 pages of data. This is going to be a really heavy book with very, very boring content. It is not much fun to take this with you on holiday. Now someone might come up with the idea of shortening the whole thing to: '75,600 × (Data is not information—it must be interpreted)'. So, this one line has the same informational content as the book, which would be extremely easier, but would probably remain just as boring. On the other hand, both volumes of the 1972 Hamburg telephone book could be printed on these 1500 pages. All phone numbers of a city are then not only data, but also information in a book that is certainly just as boring—but you can't shorten it as much.

Let's get back to Big Data. You do not need data for the application, but meaningful information. And a whole lot of it.

Example

If we want to apply this insight for an optimal suggestion algorithm in an online shop for glasses, we need the following data of the person visiting our shop:

- the gender,
- the age,
- the fashion preference and style,
- the body and head size,
- the shape of the head,
- the hairstyle and
- the hair colour

The more precisely we know all these factors and combine them into a proposal using the right algorithms, the more precisely we can predict whether the customer will wear these glasses in the future, that is, whether he or she will buy them!

If data is missing or even if only some of this data is incorrect, this could lead to an automatic prediction that is extremely wrong. Let's just assume that the age was missing or wrong: 8 instead of 38 years. A 38-year-old female lawyer would probably not be particularly willing to buy glasses designed for 8-year-old girls if they were offered to her. If you go through the above list, bizarre examples can immediately come to mind for each wrong match: men who are fitted with women's glasses, missing head size leads to people with small heads wearing oversized glasses, etc. ◀

So, data needs to not just be correct, but complete as well. This requirement for completeness is, by the way, the current problem of many elections researchers, who have been wrong in many important elections in recent years, despite years of applying sophisticated big-data techniques and after long periods of success. As some numerically relevant groups of voters were socially ostracised before the election, such as Brexit opponents in the UK or Trump fans in the USA, these groups simply gave wrong answers in polls on voting preferences. The corresponding group was then clearly undervalued in the analysis and the predicted result was frighteningly out of touch with reality. Even with more data, you won't be able to cope with such problems, because groups that are not represented in the research will always cause prediction problems.

▶ Big Data is already suffering from the mass of data, not only in intelligence agencies, but also in many companies today, which threatens to stifle the procurers of this data.

Hurdle 2: The Pattern in the Noise
To turn data into information, connections must be extracted from a confusing number of bits and bytes, from so-called noise, which is what large data collections are at first. Even despite systems capable of learning, this is only possible to a very limited extent with machines. Although we can easily determine correlations of different data strands, that is, the similarity of the growth curves, mathematically, there is no mathematical solution for whether such similar growth curves really depend logically on one another or not, that is, whether they are causal.

Example

There are clearly recognisable statistical correlations between

- the economic value of a pop star and the number of his/her fans on social media platforms,
- the frequency of mosquito bites and the use of sunscreen,
- the number of storks and the birth rate in Europe (Matthews 2001),
- the maximum daily temperature of a year and the consumption of ice cream.

But obviously there is no causal connection in the second and third example—the value pairs do not depend on each other at all (and for the very young readers among us: no, in the third example there is definitely no connection!)

Even in the first example, it is not possible to deduce from the correlation which part is causal and which is consequential. Do pop stars have many fans because they are successful—or are they successful because they have so many fans?

Such logic relationships, which go beyond mere similarities of the curves, can only be determined to a very limited extent by a machine. Big data systems therefore urgently need the work of highly competent analysts who try to recognise patterns in data from which rules for automatic evaluations can be derived. So, such systems need someone in front of the PC to decide whether storks and babies have anything to do with each other and whether the fans are a consequence of the success. This is the analyst—a human being! ◀

Now, the recognition of patterns is a very special topic for us as humans, as we will see in Chap. 2. Especially as descendants of Stone Age people fixated on the pattern of the sabre-toothed tiger, we have difficulty not seeing a predator behind every bush. We tend to see patterns where there are none.

Please read this sentence once:

A SPARROW IN THE
THE HAND IS BETTER
THAN A DOVE ON THE ROOF

If you were a big-data analyst, you might have initially recognised this sentence as a meaningful pattern—you can assign meaning to the letters. However, you would also have to recognise the inconsistency in this apparent pattern and then remove the corresponding data from an evaluation.

What inconsistency? You didn't notice anything? Perhaps you need to read the sentence again?[3]

► Patterns are both the greatest blessing and the biggest problem of big-data analysis. We need them for data analysis, but only want them if they are actual, meaningful patterns.

Hurdle 3: Again the Event Funnel

We already talked about the event funnel: looking into the future is somehow comparable with looking into the distance. The closer something you look at is, the more precisely you can recognise it—the further away you look, the less clear it becomes. Big Data also suffers from this problem. The more accurately you want to predict something—and the longer your desired time horizon is—the more data you need to collect, evaluate and understand.

Although the mass data usage in online shopping systems is actually already much better than the estimates of earlier systems, we are still miles away from reasonably reliable predictions even on a very short time horizon. My daughter, for example, lives in The Netherlands, and a single package bought at Amazon and sent as a gift still leads to Amazon offering me the Dutch start page of the shop every time. Ever since I once visited a client's website via Google, the search engine giant has been tracking me with their online advertising. Does that really make us sure that these systems can predict our behaviour, at close range at least?

A few years ago, Google boasted that it could predict waves of flu thanks to its analysis methods. However, a control study by scientists David Lazer and Alessandro Vespignani of Northeastern University revealed that a wave of influenza in 2009 had been overlooked and in the following years the extent of the seasonal epidemics was completely overestimated. Between 2011 and 2013, the

[3] The solution: one word in this sentence appears twice. Please check again.

tool delivered over-forecasts in 100 out of 108 weeks (Lazer et al. 2014). This, by the way, is exactly the reason why Google reacted very narrowly when US President Trump announced at an early stage of the Corona crisis in March 2020 (Koetsier 2020) that the company would use an algorithm to predict the exact course of the pandemic. Up to the time this book went to press, Google—although certainly the largest data collector in the world—had not made any further comments.

If you would like to check it out yourself with a less business-oriented example, just look at the results of the European Song Contest—also predicted by Google. While the forecasts for the 2009 and 2010 (for German readers: The Lena year!) competition were correct, the search engine giant was so off track in 2011 (the second Lena year) that they stopped official predictions for the following years. Google saw Lena in first place again and the Italian entry by Raphael Guallazzi (you don't have to remember the name) in 25th place. The result was, Lena ended up in seventh place and the Italian in second place.

To see how good or bad Google's prediction results were, Bernd created five additional, purely randomly generated "result lists" and calculated, for these and for the Google prediction, the average deviation of each participant's place from the final result. A catastrophic result for the globe's biggest data analyst: four of the five randomly generated lists were closer to the final result than Google's prediction (Fig. 1.6).

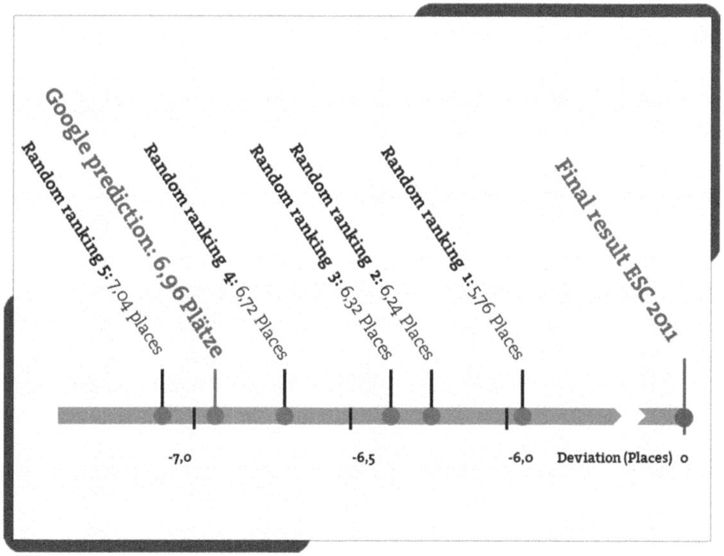

Fig. 1.6 Quality of Google prediction on ESC 2011 compared to randomly generated rankings. (Data source: www.zeit-und-wahrheit.de)

So, under scientific rules, it must be said that Google's seemingly accurate results for 2009 and 2010 were actually no more than pure coincidence. There is also no chance of improvement: Two renewed attempts in 2016 and 2017 also failed.

Not to be misunderstood: Big Data solutions can, when used correctly, already deliver many extraordinary results today. Image and face recognition, reading body language and interpreting weather data is already possible today in a quality that our ancestors would have envied 20 years ago. And certainly, commercial applications with a very-short-term view are already well implemented in some places today. But Big Data is still light years away from making meaningful, credible forecasts about the future, even in the short-term.

So, how Far Can forecasts Be Trusted?

There are no real forecasts for the future for a wide variety of reasons and, as we have seen, there never will be. If you believe otherwise, here is a quote from Philip Tetlock, who had analysed 20 years of expert forecasts (Tetlock and Gardner 2016, p. 55):

> The prognoses of the twenty first century is all too often reminiscent of nineteenth century medicine. There are theories, assertions and arguments galore. Some famous luminaries provide certainty to the extent that they are paid for it. But there are hardly any experiments or anything that resembles science in the broadest sense, which is why we know much less about the future than most people suspect.

However, that doesn't mean you have to be idle.

- For example, if you were a fashion retailer, you can go to great lengths to optimise your offer and encourage customers to make further purchases. However, planning for the next 3 to 5 years makes no sense in this way.
- If you pay attention to the retrospective errors (see Sect. 2.3), you can also massively increase your forecasting with simple means and a little Excel and thus, for example, significantly improve your cash flow.
- And if you build your planning process with an "operational elasticity", you can actually prepare for the future to some extent. How this works is the subject of Chaps. 5 to 7.

1.8 The Flock, the Flock Bird and the Consultant

Anyone who has the opportunity in autumn to experience a large flock of birds flying may be fascinated by the harmonious geometry of the whole flock. The seemingly perfectly staged choreography, by which the flock changes its figure, is a feast for the eyes. And of course, the movements of these flocks have always been an attraction for scientists all over the world who wish to describe them, particularly using mathematical models.

Such a movement model for flocks and swarms is a typical Big Data problem. Extremely large amounts of data from individual birds are analysed until an idea emerges of how to describe their behaviour. Data-based forecasting models with which the mail order companies Otto, Amazon or Zalando manage their online business work exactly according to this principle, because markets do indeed behave in a similar way to swarms.

Economics—mathematics—biology, everything somehow belongs together. And so it is not surprising that it was a professor of quantum physics, Giorgio Parisi, who succeeded in mapping swarm behaviour with his model. In fact, Parisi is one of the pioneers of numerical computer-aided science.

One very special aspect of his model is of particular interest to the business community. While the movements of the swarm can be tracked from the outside, the question arises as to whether someone in the swarm actually knows where they are going. Is the individual bird aware of where the flock is heading? And does it actively contribute to the course finding of the swarm?

This is of course a strange-sounding question when you only look at birds. However, when one realises that many processes in the economy and society are based on similar algorithms, the question takes on a very important meaning: If I am part of an industry or a market, can I fully comprehend the movement of the swarm from this internal position? And to what extent do I control, or at least contribute to, the movement of the market. Am I, myself, being controlled?

Parisi's calculations suggest that the individual bird only pays attention to its immediate neighbours during flight and aligns its flight path accordingly (Cavagna et al. 2009). It does not perceive the absolute flight direction of the swarm or even actively control it. In other words, the bird has tunnel vision!

Let's take a moment to consider what this means for managers. By focusing on the immediate neighbours—the competitors—you run the risk of losing sight of the big picture. So, if a bird—as part of a flock—wants to find out where the flock is going, it should become a "marginal bird". Or, even better, it should fly out of the swarm from time to time and look at it from the outside.

The same is true for managers. They need an unbiased view. A helicopter perspective, so to speak. But to be able to take on such a perspective, one first needs the insight that flock birds tend to have tunnel vision. Sounds a bit like that famous cat biting its own tail, doesn't it? In my opinion, this is exactly the point where many management mistakes actually start, because nothing seems to be more difficult for successful managers than the realisation that they cannot have an objective view of their own business. If you confront managers with this thesis, you often reap vigorous protest: 'After 20 years of experience in this industry, there is surely no one who understands this industry better than me!'

Yes, there is! Someone who doesn't fly in a swarm, but can give you the outside view. Someone who has the necessary know-how; but does not exclude views, solutions or entire solution approaches on the basis of daily practice within a company; can open up completely different approaches to your market and the market participants. Please remember: in most industries, the customers are not market experts and therefore have a completely different view of the market than the suppliers.

Such freethinkers in your future project could be employees who have not been involved up to now in the strategy process. Or external consultants. Let me therefore point out once again that you should definitely include a good cross-section of your company in your future process. You wouldn't believe what exciting contributions the employee from the finance department or the lady from the B2B product area could make to strategic considerations in the B2C area, if you just would let them!

However, it must be remembered that some routines and working methods that have developed in the company over many years of practice can have a limiting effect on the entire company, even the uninvolved financier or marketer of the B2B sector. People, and with that companies, usually prefer certain ways and procedures for discussing something. There is a preferred place to be creative, and there is a preferred method for brainstorming, which may no longer work simply because the brain has been washed too often in this way. On the other hand, certain methods may be foregone, because they "do not fit our organisation".

Does this look familiar to you? If so, you should consider whether such routines might block your way. And then, as difficult as it may be for you, you should perhaps consider he who cannot be named… the external *consultant*.

Oops, I named him!

As I said, consultants have a rather limited positive image among managers. If this job title immediately brings to mind the (perceived) billions of graduates who are sent by some consulting firms as "junior somethings" in projects to fill in PowerPoint slides and project sheets, it will be difficult to involve consultants in the strategic process. Even serious, experienced consultants quickly arouse resistance with views of the market that conflict with the experiences of the internal managers involved. It is precisely at this point, however, that it is important for strategy development to look at such alternative perspectives and to critically review its own view time and again. Consultants—if they are well-chosen—have the potential to act as catalysts for a new way of thinking in the future planning process.

▶ Be sure to think about how you might expand your future management to include this outside perspective.

References

Adidas (2015) Maßgeschneidert aus dem 3-D-Drucker: Erschaffe Deinen individuellen Laufschuh. https://www.adidas-group.com/de/medien/newsarchiv/pressemitteilungen/2015/massgeschneidert-aus-dem-3d-drucker-erschaffe-deinen-individuell/. Zugegriffen: 20. Mai 2020

Becker J (2017) Intelligente Vernetzung könnte jeden dritten Unfall verhindern. http://www.sueddeutsche.de/auto/verkehrssicherheit-zu-viele-unfalltote-trotz-sicherer-autos-1.3536640-2. Zugegriffen: 20. Mai 2020

Berry M (1978) Regular and irregular motion. https://michaelberryphysics.files.wordpress.com/2013/07/berry076.pdf#page=1&zoom=auto,-277,841. Zugegriffen: 20. Mai 2020

Bundesministerium der Justiz und für Verbraucherschutz (2017) Straßenverkehrsgesetz (StVG). https://www.gesetze-im-internet.de/stvg/BJNR004370909.html. Zugegriffen: 11. Mai 2020

Cavagna A, Cimarelli A, Giardina I, Parisi G (2009) Scale-free correlations in starling flocks. http://www.pnas.org/content/107/26/11865.full. Zugegriffen: 11. Mai 2020

CIPA (2020) Digital Cameras Statisticaal Data. http://www.cipa.jp/stats/dc_e.html. Zugegriffen: 18. Mai 2020

Dale AI, Laplace P-S (1995) Pierre-Simon laplace philosophical essay on probabilities: translated from the fifth French edition of 1825. Springer, Berlin

DARPA (2007) DARPA Urban Challenge. https://www.darpa.mil/about-us/timeline/darpa-urban-challenge. Zugegriffen: 18. Mai 2020

DPD (2019) Daten & Fakten Das Elektrofahrzeug StreetScooter. https://www.dpdhl.com/content/dam/dpdhl/de/media-center/media-relations/documents/2019/fact-sheet-street-scooter-yamato-de.pdf. Zugegriffen: 12. Mai 2020

Erhardt B (2011) Falsche Prognosen von Google: Eurovision Song Contest 2011. http://www.zeit-und-wahrheit.de/falsche-prognosen-von-google-eurovision-song-contest-2011-4692/. Zugegriffen: 18. Mai 2020

Frey T (2017) 25 shocking predictions about the coming driverless car era in the U.S. https://futuristspeaker.com/predictions/25-shocking-predictions-about-the-coming-driverless-car-era-in-the-u-s/. Zugegriffen: 2. Jun 2020

Focus Online (2016) Die bittere Wahrheit: Das Elektroauto vernichtet Arbeitsplätze. http://www.focus.de/auto/elektroauto/auto-vw-personalchef-werk-salzgitter-braucht-neue-aufgaben_id_5930673.html. Zugegriffen: 18. Mai 2020

Hamburger Hochbahn (2020) Projekt HEAT: HOCHBAHN-Forschungsprojekt zu automatisiert fahrenden Kleinbussen. https://www.hochbahn.de/hochbahn/hamburg/de/Home/Naechster_Halt/Ausbau_und_Projekte/projekt_heat. Zugegriffen: 12. Mai 2020

Herger M (2018) Der letzte Führerscheinneuling ist schon geboren. Börsen Medien AG, Kulmbach

Johnson S (2018) How to make a big decision. https://www.nytimes.com/2018/09/01/opinion/sunday/how-make-big-decision.html. Zugegriffen: 15. Mai 2020

Koetsier J (2020) Trump: 1,700 google engineers working on coronavirus site. Google says … actually, no. https://www.forbes.com/sites/johnkoetsier/2020/03/13/trump-1700-google-engineers-working-on-coronavirus-site-google-says–actually-no/#2a8fa21b54cc. Zugegriffen: 15. Mai 2020

Lazer D, Kennedy R, King G, Vespignani A (2014) The parable of google flu: traps in big data analysis. http://science.sciencemag.org/content/343/6176/1203. Zugegriffen: 10. Aug 2020

Maastricht University (2017) Cultured meat. https://culturedbeef.org/. Zugegriffen: 20. Mai 2020

Matthews R (2001) Der Storch bringt die Babys zur Welt. http://www3.math.uni-paderborn.de/~agbiehler/sis/sisonline/struktur/jahrgang21-2001/heft2/Langfassungen/2001-2_Matth.pdf. Zugegriffen: 18. Mai 2020

Memphis Meats (2017) Announcing the world's first chicken produced without the animal. http://www.memphismeats.com/. Zugegriffen: 18. Mai 2020

Peters TJ, Waterman RH (1986) Auf der Suche nach Spitzenleistungen. Moderne Industrie, Landsberg

Phantastische Bibliothek Wetzlar (2020) Future Life in der Presse. https://www.phantastik.eu/pressespiegel/future-life-in-der-presse.html. Zugegriffen: 18. Mai 2020

Poppe H (2020) Zukunftsforscher Matthias Horx glaubt nicht an Leben auf anderen Planeten. https://www.frankfurt-live.com/zukunftsforscher-matthias-horx-glaubt-nicht-an-leben-auf-anderen-planeten-118774.html. Zugegriffen: 12. Mai 2020

Rosenzweig P (2014) The Halo effect: … and the eight other Business delusions that deceive managers. Simon & Schuster, New York

Samsung (2020) Samsung presents groundbreaking all-solid-state battery technology to 'nature energy'. https://news.samsung.com/global/samsung-presents-groundbreaking-all-solid-state-battery-technology-to-nature-energy. Zugegriffen: 14. Mai 2020

Santoso A (2008) The stupidest business decisions in history. http://www.neatorama.com/2008/04/15/the-stupidest-Business-decisions-in-history/. Zugegriffen: 14. Mai 2020

Schalk R (2016) Meat the future. http://www.faz.net/aktuell/stil/essen-trinken/kuenstliches-fleisch-der-burger-aus-der-petrischale-14030839.html. Zugegriffen: 20. Mai 2020

Spiegel (2019) Jedes dritte neugeborene Mädchen wird 100 Jahre alt. https://www.spiegel.de/gesundheit/diagnose/deutschland-jedes-dritte-neugeborene-maedchen-wird-100-a-1263975.html. Zugegriffen: 12. Mai 2020

Statista (2020) Anzahl der Tankstellen in Deutschland von 1950 bis 2020. https://de.statista.com/statistik/daten/studie/2621/umfrage/anzahl-der-tankstellen-in-deutschland-zeitreihe/. Zugegriffen: 12. Mai 2020

Stehle A (2017) Der Mann, der Volkswagen als Digitalchef retten soll. https://m.abendblatt.de/wirtschaft/article211232659/Der-Mann-der-Volkswagen-als-Digitalchef-retten-soll.html. Zugegriffen: 12. Mai 2020

SuperMeat (2017). http://www.supermeat.com. Zugegriffen: 18. Mai 2020

Tetlock PE, Gardner D (2016) Superforecasting–Die Kunst der richtigen Prognose. Fischer, Frankfurt a. M

VW (2019) Laser, Radar, Ultraschall: Autonomes Fahren in Hamburg. https://www.volkswagenag.com/de/news/stories/2019/04/laser-radar-ultrasound-autonomous-driving-in-hamburg.html. Zugegriffen: 12. Mai 2020

Zitt H (2013) Technologien aus Star Trek: Jeder Schüler hat ein besseres Handy als Captain Kirk. http://www.focus.de/digital/technologien-aus-star-trek-jeder-schueler-hat-ein-besseres-handy-als-captain-kirk_id_3442718.html. Zugegriffen: 12. Mai 2020

2 Eight Typical Thinking Errors

Abstract

Every manager, every entrepreneur and every futurologist is inevitably subject to many human thinking errors and mistakes when assessing the future—learned errors, gaps in imagination or ways of thinking that have been genetically consolidated over generations. But those who are aware of these thinking traps can consciously avoid them in strategy development. In fact, there are dozens of such traps—you will learn about the eight most important ones in this chapter.

These days, a document of the German Robert Koch Institute emerged, in which the institute describes a virtual virus in risk analysis for the Bundestag already in 2012, which seems to be very similar to the Corona pathogen and its worldwide consequences (Deutscher Bundestag 2012). Other countries such as the USA or the UK also had such early warnings. So could the pandemic have been prevented if someone would have listened?

Well, we will deal with this in more detail in Sect. 2.3—just this much in advance: This way of thinking is typically a result of the so-called *retrospective bias*. Do you remember the thing about our view of the past? Surely it is easy for us today to recognize the mistakes of previous generations as such. Only the other way round—i.e., to look from today into the future—is still as difficult or even impossible as it was for our ancestors. One way to improve this is through appropriate systematic preparation. But even with this, unfortunately, we are always subject to fatal errors in thinking in this process, which can easily lead to such preparations

H. Hilbig, *Shaping the Future of Your Business*,
https://doi.org/10.1007/978-3-658-35349-0_2

ad absurdum. Incidentally, this is a problem from which even scientists and politicians are not immune!

We will now take a closer look at the most important of these thinking traps. If you consciously avoid these mistakes repeatedly, you have the chance to transfer your company into a promising future. However, this requires an openness that your organization and you as a managing director or department head must bring with you: You must be willing to accept that your market will look different in the future than you experience it today. If you cling to the idea that everything will remain as it is today, you are not only mistaken. You may risk the future viability of your organization.

2.1 Bias 1: The Linear View of Time

One of the most dangerous phrases related to planning for the future came from a CEO I once worked with: "When change comes, we adapt. We are so flexible that we can change our business at any time." This colleague, who is unfortunately not alone in his view, was firmly convinced that changes in his market—and his competitors and customers—would give him time to adapt the company to them.

Now, it is almost a truism when articles on the subject of planning for the future point out that technological changes in particular are taking place ever more rapidly. The term "exponential increase" is usually used in this context. Most of us may still darkly remember this chapter from math or physics class, the formula (e^x) and, at least since the counting of the infected in the virus crisis, the steeply rising curve. The only problem is that we simply cannot imagine what this means! We humans tend to perceive change linearly. "We tend to think quasistatically and in terms of linear causality," is how the honorary president of the German Society of the Club of Rome, Michael F. Jischa (2009), describes it. We have experienced the past and the changes taking place in it in a linear sequence and expect the same for the future. Now, when someone talks about future changes being rather faster (though not exponential, by the way!), we can recall the chart with the steep upward arc, but imagine what that means in reality—no, we can't imagine it. So let's try again to help with a thought experiment:

Example

Let's say you were to take 20 linear steps, and let's assume 75cm as the step size—then you would have covered about 15m after 20 steps. That's about the distance you cover at the crosswalk of a four-lane road. Now guess where you would end up if you could take exponential steps. The first step would be 75cm long and each subsequent step would be longer according to exponential growth. Please take a guess! You'll find the resolution in the footnote[1].

I'm sure you didn't estimate that distance, right? At least no one in my lectures has ever estimated further than let's say the nearest town.

Now we transfer this picture back to temporal distances and market changes. Everything happens much faster than you think: Serious changes to your market don't expect to happen for another 20 or 30 years, but then they come in as little as five. In the face of such rapid changes, can you be sure that you will be able to adapt to this tsunami of events and change your business model in time without any preparations? I honestly don't think so. ◄

But the speed at which markets change is only one aspect that makes short-term strategy changes rarely successful. The other is that in a crisis you simply need too long to bring a new strategy or a new product to market. Please take a look at the chart in Fig. 2.1.

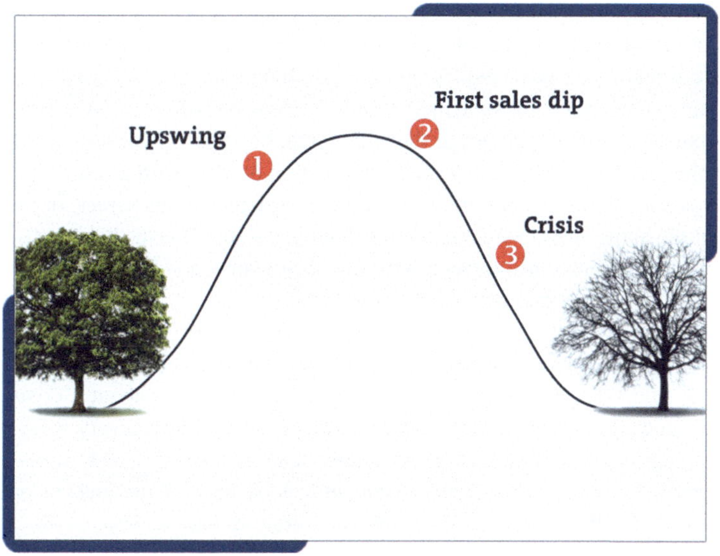

Fig. 2.1 Growth curve of a typical life cycle

[1] After 20 steps they would have covered 363,874. kilometers and would thus - at least as far as distance is concerned - land approximately on the moon.

The curve is statistically a typical lifetime curve of a product, brand or even an entire market segment. The life of the product starts on the left, peaks in the middle (becoming a cash cow), before plunging into the fall and winter of its life on the right. Let's assume this is a company's most important product category. What typically happens in the company at different points of time?

Phase 1 The company is very busy enjoying the success of the product genre and continuing to expand it through ever new measures. The product is the rising star. At this point, no one can or wants to think about what will come after this product category—which will then secure the company's sales, profits and jobs—because all the capable and powerful employees are busy working for the further expansion of the successful category.

Phase 2 The product category has peaked and just passed its peak. Sales and profits start to shrink only slightly at first, but permanently. Unfortunately, only no one in the company knows this. The slight decline is thought to be a temporary dip in sales. An experienced sales manager has had exactly this experience before and now acts accordingly. All the old familiar methods of how to classically dent sales dips are brought out: price reductions, special offers, bundles, an additional direct marketing campaign, longer payment terms, ten-plus-one offers … well, you know it all yourself. Even though one or the other might think so, no one will openly talk about the fact that the company might not just be dealing with a sales dip, especially, as something like that may have quickly a demotivating effect. In the end, none of the above mentioned measures will help, because it is the beginning of the market change. But at the moment, only you, dear reader, and I, who are looking at Fig. 2.1 from a helicopter perspective, know this.

Phase 3 At some point, the brand or the product has reached this point. Now the company and sales management can no longer avoid talking about a crisis. The turnover goes down permanently and decreases more and more every week. Now countermeasures have to be taken: A creative team is formed, which meets every fortnight in an empty office in the basement to look for new products or product segments that will carry the company into the future. At the same time, cost-cutting measures are decided upon, since the lack of sales naturally affects the company's bottom line. Marketing is cut back. New positions are only filled internally for the time being or even left open altogether. In the next phase, the first employees are sent into early retirement …

You probably know such processes yourself. A Japanese friend once described this situation in his company to me very aptly with the words: "We are in panic mode. They were in panic mode because none of the known remedies were working anymore and the downfall felt unstoppable.

Put yourself in the shoes of the 14-day creative team in the basement for a moment. Have the best minds in the company been assembled there, or rather those who are most likely to be dispensed with on the sales front in "these difficult times"? And how creative can this team still be? How "big" can it still think? Which ideas are still feasible with the shrinking budgets? Now let's assume that the creative team does find something, has an idea that can be implemented with limited investment, and the company can quickly decide on it—which is not a given in panic mode—then we would again have a growth curve for the new product (Fig. 2.2).

The picture says it all: before the new idea can make an impact and generate sales, the company has long been in a downward spiral, and the results of the new product do not compensate for the losses. So what chance does a company have of making up for a change in the market with a new product if they only start thinking about it when the crisis has already arrived? None!

If you want to prepare your company for such changes, you have to start as long as these market changes are not yet acute and as long as your degrees of freedom and budgets allow such processes (Fig. 2.2).

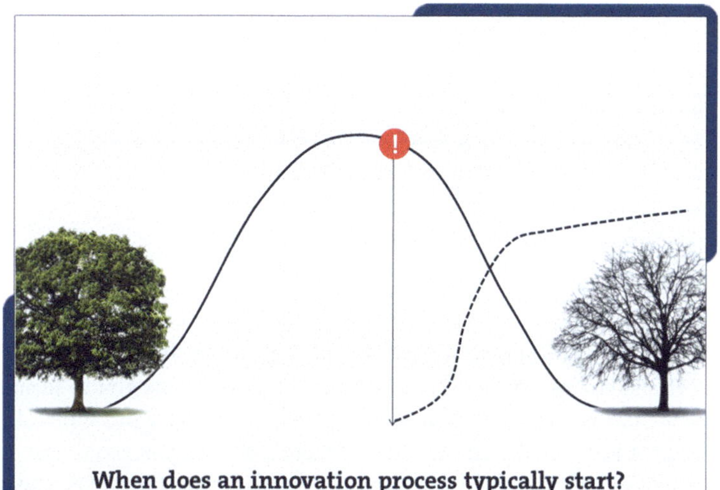

Fig. 2.2 Growth curve of the substitute product

▶ Are you and your business doing well right now? Okay, then now is the time to prepare for a different future!

2.2 Bias 2: Compulsive Pattern Recognition

If you have thought for a moment about the self-experiment in Sect. 1.4, you may have quickly concluded that your daily routine, no matter how monotonous your day promises to be, depends on so many coincidences that a reliable prediction is actually impossible. You conclude this from your experience, because yesterday, too, many things happened by chance. For example, the colleague you met by chance in the canteen who gave you a valuable hint for your current project (and thus changed the timing for this project), the PC crash that blocked you for 20 minutes or the phone call from your life partner that caused you to work shorter hours than usual. All unpredictable!

Nevertheless, even though the past of your company, your industry and society as a whole was also built from many coincidences, we try to recognize a pattern in it and thus plan for the future. Strictly speaking, we can't help it, because our brains are programmed to recognize patterns in everyone and everything. Just think of the famous Rorschach inkblot test, where you are asked about a (definitely random!) inkblot and what you see in it.

A Small Task

In the following series of numbers, find the next two logically following numbers in that series and the rule behind them.

1, 6, 7, 10, 11, 12, 16.

Please think about this for a minute!

Have you found them? What is the law of the series and the next two values? Well, here comes the solution: 1, 6, 7, 10, 11, 12, 16, ***22, 30.*** Do you have other values? Hmm, strange. What exactly is the rule that you think you've identified? Because the fact is, I had a random number generator given me this series of numbers and then just sorted them by size. So there's no way you could have found those numbers—the only "correct" rule would have been that the next two numbers had to be greater than 16. So if you found a different logic and came up with two numbers as a suggested solution, then you were looking for a pattern in a purely random data series and you found it. Congratulations! But quite obviously you let me lead you up the garden path …

This effect accompanies us throughout our lives. We always look for patterns in everything and use them to explain the world to ourselves: we know that non-calculable chance determines our lives in many areas, but we place the chips in the casino according to rules we have invented ourselves. "If red came 20 times, black must follow now." No. Must not! You will lose your bet with a 51.3% chance![2] And that probability doesn't change whether red came five times before, 20 times or 250 times.

The cause of all this mishap is our ancestors, who were successful in evolutionary history. Those who could quickly recognize a pattern with as little information as possible could then act faster—run away, for example, if the pattern turned out to be a saber-toothed tiger. And those who took a little longer became tiger food and, due to sudden death, were unable to pass on their genes to anyone. Therefore, you and I—and all the people around us—are descendants of the pattern recognizers.

Being able to quickly recognize patterns in complex systems was thus a clear survival advantage and has become second nature to us, so to speak: Decisions that could be evaluated according to a pattern and (above all) had to be done quickly were outsourced to our subconscious. To think about the existence of a saber-toothed tiger consciously would simply take too long and would also consume valuable energy because the brain is also the largest energy consumer of our body! Even if we wanted to, we cannot turn off this subconscious pattern. Once we have learned a pattern, we inevitably always use it to assess a current situation (or to evaluate the future).

Please take a look at the picture in Fig. 2.3 and take a minute to look at it. Can you see anything in it? What do you see? I'm going to guess that you see as much on it as you do on the inkblot tests. You could read something into it if you really wanted to. But you probably did not see anything concrete, did you?

Now please look at Fig. 2.4. on page 48. Now it suddenly becomes much clearer. You have recognized the pattern, haven't you?

Finally, the third part of the self-awareness: Please look again at the picture in Fig. 2.3. You now recognise the motif even without the assistance, don't you? But: Can you recognize something else than the stored pattern? Can you

[2] Out of 37 squares on the roulette table, 19 lose if you bet on black.

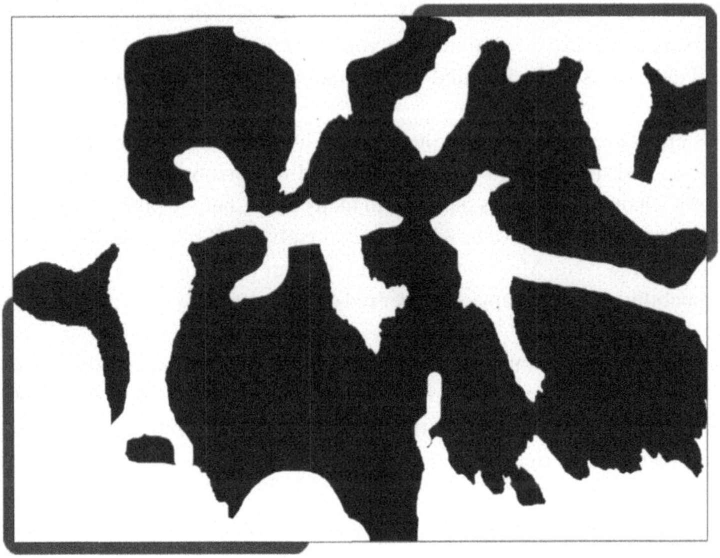

Fig. 2.3 Can you recognize any familiar pattern on it?

switch off the pattern now stored in your brain? No. You can no longer help seeing the two cows.

Once we have stored a pattern, it becomes irretrievably the basis of every future judgment. Therefore, I could be sure that most of you would not recognize the example in Sect. 1.7 ("A bird in the hand…") at first reading, because you know the saying: You always judge, like all people by the way, with the familiar patterns.

We can practically no longer judge without bias. So that's exactly why our preferred method of prediction is to reach into possibly known structures of the past. What's crazy is that this even plays out when we want to consciously look for a "non-pattern", i.e., chance.

Example

Think about a lottery for a moment. At the most popular German lottery ("Lotto 6 aus 49") 6 balls are chosen from a total of 49. We all know that the numbers fall purely by chance and that every pick has an equal chance of being drawn of about 1 in 13 million. But ask your friends or colleagues if they would put their money on the tip *"1 – 2 – 3-4 – 5 – 6"*. Most of them will indignantly refuse—even though this tip is not one bit less likely than any other. Such winning numbers must look "random"—and we evaluate this again using a pattern which we think we have "recognized" in the weekly drawing of the lottery numbers. There, a sequence of six consecutive numbers never occurs as a result (I only hope that this does not happen now, of all times, after the publication of this book!) So we have a picture of how random numbers should look like and therefore evaluate the combination *1-2 – 3-4 – 5-6* as "not random"—and thus as a more improbable lottery tip. ◄

We look for patterns in past events, whether these patterns are valid or not, and interpolate them into the future. Yet we know intuitively that this method cannot be correct: If in a lottery draw the numbers 1–2–3-4-5 were drawn one after the other—and in exactly this order—we would never assume that the next number would be a 6—although this would be exactly the logical pattern …

And what does that mean for your strategic planning?

► If you think you have recognized a pattern in the market activity of your company in the past, do not conclude from this under any circumstances the development in the future—the apparently recognized pattern could have been a pure coincidence!

2.3 Bias 3: The Hindsight Bias

At the beginning of Chap. 2, I already mentioned the study of the German Robert Kochs Institute, which had been prepared at the end of 2012 for the German parliament *Bundestag* as a risk analysis. So could a large part of the suffering caused by Corona—at least in Germany—have been avoided if the politicians had read this report and acted accordingly? Well, the answer to that must be "yes", because all the fears listed in the report, such as insufficient supplies of face masks and protective clothing, then come true during the pandemic worldwide at the beginning of 2020.

But much more exciting is the question of whether the politicians could have recognized the importance of this forecast. And here I am much more cautious in my assessment. Because predictions (i.e., singular statements about a possible situation in the future) are a dime a dozen. For the Bundestag alone, the Robert Koch Institute officially produced six risk analyses between 2012 and 2016:

- Extreme melt floods from the low mountain ranges (2012)
- Virus Modi-SARS pandemic (2012)
- Winter Storm (2013)

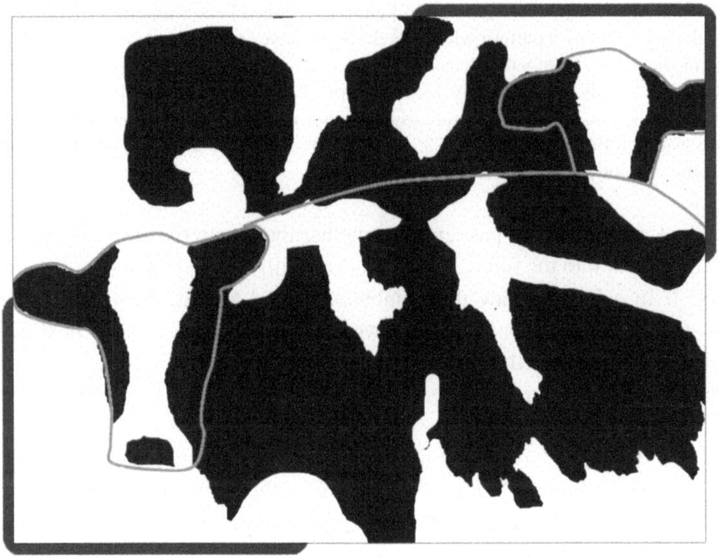

Fig. 2.4 Did you recognize it?

- Storm surge (2014)
- Release of radioactive substances from a nuclear power plant (2015)
- Chemical Release (2016).

If you add to this all the economic institutes, university professors, lobbyists, self-proclaimed experts and "futurologists"—both national and international—the number of disastrous future expectations becomes legion. And that unfortunately devalues the individual prediction:

Example

Imagine for a moment that you are standing in a hall in front of a basket with a thousand balls. Each ball has a number printed on it and can thus be distinguished from all the other balls. You draw from this basket the ball—let's say—525. Now a person approaches you and hands you a closed and previously sealed envelope with a prediction. You open this and find the following message, "You will draw the ball with the number 525." That sounds mysterious. This person has predicted the right ball out of a thousand. A magician! You are looking for a reliable consultant? Hire him or her!

Or did he? Because if 10,000 people were sitting in the hall, each of whom had deposited a tip in an envelope, then statistically speaking, this person had only tipped the right number by chance. ◀

So if there are many divergent opinions and forecasts on a topic, according to pure probability theory there will be someone who guesses the right course. But did that person know what was coming? Did the lottery winner last week know the numbers or was he just the lucky guy?

We look for a pattern in the past and then build explanations to logically explain what happened. Many of our forecasts of the future adopt such logic to justify the expected future. As economist and Nobel laureate Robert Shiller says (Tetlock and Gardner 2016, p. 164), "We like to think that history has a logic that could have been anticipated. But it doesn't. It's an illusion that comes only in retrospect."

We look at someone who has been very successful in the past and therefore buy his book "How to become a billionaire and US president in 100 days". The logic of his book sounds compelling—that's exactly how you have to do it—after all, he did it. After all, the fact that he's president today, proves he's right ... doesn't it? You probably won't be very surprised if hardly any of the book buyers become billionaires later on. And even fewer go on to become president of the United States. But of course, we assume that it was then due to the lack of skills of the book buyers that the principle didn't work. They simply don't have what he has ... Yet there's a pretty good chance that the recipe for success isn't one at all—that's why it doesn't work—and that all his success was a fluke.

Another Nobel Prize winner should have his say at this point. Daniel Kahneman, who received the Nobel Prize in Economics as a psychologist, has proven that our brain wants certainty at any price. And if there is no certainty, it is invented. This is how myths are created around past successes.

Using a slightly modified example from my first book *Marketing ist eine Wissenschaft* (Marketing is a science) ... (Hilbig 2013), this addiction of the human brain can be well explained.

Example

To do this, imagine you encounter a man at the exit of a Las Vegas casino, carrying out masses of dollar bills in two large plastic bags. The people around you tell you that he won all that money in a tough seven-hour battle at the poker table. He was the winner of that marathon round.

What will you think of this man now? Exactly, that he must be a really good poker player. Am I about right in that assessment?

Well, let's change the scenario now: You are now met in the casino by a chimpanzee with big bags filled with … well, you know. The scenario is exactly the same: Seven hours of poker played. All bluffed out, and so on. What are you thinking now? Do you still think you just ran into one of the coolest poker players in town? You're not changing your basic mindset based on objective facts but your apparent prior knowledge. Let's take a look at the game:

The winning monkey sat at the poker table with a whole bunch of chimps for seven hours. Cards were dealt and everyone had the same amount of chips available as well as a box with three buttons in front of them to fold, call or raise. Let's further assume that we had failed to even begin to explain the idea of the game to the primates: Their animal counterparts were tapping the buttons on the machine in a completely content-less and purely random manner. Nevertheless—such are the rules of this game: In the end, one of the monkeys had won the first round and a fancy stack of chips, and the others had lost part of their capital.

After a few games, the first one got it—no more chips, the monkey was broke and eliminated. The rest continued to play: little by little, more and more chimpanzees left the table in frustration. Then the showdown: The last opponent hit the "all in" button on his controller and … lost. All the game chips were now stacked in front of the winner you met at the exit.

Question: Did that last monkey do anything to win, or did he just get lucky? The answer is as clear to you as it is to me: it was pure luck, of course, and the win came about because in poker players are taken out of the game as soon as the chips run out. At the end, one monkey had to win—that's how the game Poker works. Only: Which of the monkeys that would be, was completely unclear.

But then why do we presuppose in the same situation with a man that his success was something other than pure luck? Couldn't the man with the bags have just been lucky? Drawn cards and bet money purely by chance? Three years ago, when I was writing the first edition of this book, a man won the poker world championship and US$8.1 million who had come into contact with the game for the first time in his life just two years before (Spiegel Online 2017).

If we wanted to attribute scientifically correct abilities to this man that led to his victory, we would have to repeat the game a few times. If he wins again and altogether more often than average, then there could be something to it and his success could be the result of a method. However, as long as we cannot repeat and evaluate this experimental set-up, the first victory is therefore completely meaningless. This applies to chimpanzees in Las Vegas just as much as it does to the recipes for the success of billionaires/presidents or any individual prediction drawn from pure observation of the past. It is not possible to check, whether the logic of the process, resulting from the backward-view, was planned by the participants or achieved by their active performance—or whether our brain just needed certainty afterwards. ◄

Therefore, beware of retrospectively assigning logic to an event that happened once in your industry and then from there concluding the future. Although your competitor may have gained market share after increasing distribution, this may also backfire for him or any other market participant in the future. Without repeating the experiment several times, you cannot tell if there was a (predictable) relationship between the two events of "increased distribution" and "increased market share". No matter how logical that may sound.

Apple disciples will always rave to you about the founder's streak of genius—but: Did Steve Jobs really create the online platform iTunes from the start as an integral solution for his future iPhone empire—or did it just happen to evolve into that from a music download portal? We probably won't find out.

As I said, not everyone becomes a billionaire or US president after buying a promising biography. What might be the reason for that?

▶ Backward-looking errors are the most dangerous causes of false predictions: the seemingly compelling logic provides the human consciousness with the certainty we are looking for, thus blocking critical inquiry.

2.4 Bias 4: Black Swans

Once a year, I sit at my bank advisor's desk in a moderately exciting room and have her explain to me which form of investment will be the most promising in the coming year. The information has been compiled by analysts at the bank based on past data and future assessments. The exciting thing: Both my bank advisor and the analysts and even the bank's chief executive continue to work, fulfilling their respective employee contracts. This made me wonder. Billions of euros are being moved on international financial markets with unbelievable profits—and no one at my bank is quitting because of personal wealth? If my bank's tips were really convincing, wouldn't their employees have to invest all their income in it first and foremost and be infinitely wealthy by now?

The American author Peter Lynch once asked himself this question years ago and immediately answered it himself (Dobelli 2011, p. 165):

> There are about 60,000 mostly salaried financial experts in the US who are supposed to predict interest rate trends and financial crises. And if they only managed to do that twice in a row, they could all be millionaires by now. As far as I know, though, most of them are still employed, which should tell us a lot about being an expert.

Well, the thing with the financial crisis has also been unfair. Even if there are one or two people today who claim to have foreseen it back then, the world slid into misery unchecked. It just happened. Just like the Coronavirus, September 11, the invention of the PC, the Kennedy assassination, or the introduction of the first iPhone just happened and changed the world—each in its own way—abruptly.

Author and former financier Nassim Nicholas Taleb call such events "black swans"—unpredictable events that can completely change the course of events (Taleb 2014). He gave this catchy name to the phenomenon—which we all also know as "coincidence"—after people here in Europe were sure for centuries that swans would always be white. Until someone brought the first black swan from overseas. Nothing helped, neither scrubbing nor plucking—this swan remained black and destroyed a whole world view in a second.

In your self-experimentation of your daily forecast, you may have also encountered black swans: You planned to finish an important proposal, but then got a call that changed all your priorities that day. Or you were supposed to lead a field sales meeting and your computer system crashed, leaving you without a prepared PowerPoint slide to fall back on. Or—it happened to me—you're taking your family to the train, the doors close, and you cannot get off until you're 300 km away. The day's planning was gone.

Black swans have thrown the economy off course in 2020 (Coronavirus) in 2008/2009 as financial crisis, same as the touch-sensitive display knocked out Nokia in 2007. What all these events have in common is that they appear unexpectedly and cause massive changes in their respective spheres of influence.

Nassim Taleb cites the unjustified, corruption-based arrest of a single fruit trader in Tunisia, who subsequently set himself on fire in protest outside a police station, as an example of such a swan. The wave of protest swept the entire country and spread to many other states in a very short time—a process to which we in the West have given the poetic name "Arab Spring ". Skeptics of this theory then point out that this was very predictable because the corruption and oppression in these states had long since grown beyond all measure—and for the population to an unbearable degree. A typical case of retrospective bias.

So, let's check the logic:

Of course, the situation was not easy for the population. But neither was it for the 30 years before that. Why the situation tilted exactly at this time—and the misfortune of a single man then triggered the revolt of the people there—none of the backward prophets can explain.

Let's take a look at the smaller quakes of this world—back to your everyday working life: Who has not encountered black swans more often in their company or private life? Typical cases are abrupt changes in customer expectations, new technologies or products, and sudden, completely new competitors—cases of which we will look at some in more detail in Chap. 3.

Such black swans have existed at all times in the economy—and always will. They may be extremely rare, but as the virus in 2020 has shown, the probability calculation ultimately says nothing about whether and when the swan will appear. Even a low probability is not a "zero" probability. You may now say that this kind of thing only happens once every hundred years, close this book, and go about your business with a loud "Keep up the good work!". Or you could prepare yourself and your company for market changes.

▶ Unfortunately, black swans cannot be calculated by any method. However, the fact that they occur so rarely should by no means tempt you not to include such options in your future scenarios.

2.5 Bias 5: The Rules of Chaos

If you look more closely at a change, even a black swan, you usually find that there was a theoretically logical but unpredictable chain of causes:

- The Arab Spring came about because people in some Arab countries rebelled against despots.
- This happened because people in Tunisia started doing it.
- The reason for this was that a single man rebelled against the system.
- His motive for doing so was the unjust and inhumane way the local police dealt with him.

I am sure that if one were to investigate this case more intensively, completely different partial causes would emerge and every chain of reasoning could be traced back much further and deeper. If one were to try to draw all these chains of causes and their interaction on a large sheet of paper, one would have a jumble of lines against which a pattern plan from the classic women's magazine would represent a purist design.

The exciting thing about this causal research is that even the tiniest changes at the beginning can lead to completely different results later on—an outgrowth of the exponential functions that such processes often follow. But I don't want to bore you with mathematics:

Perhaps, the Tunisian fruit seller would not have resorted to such drastic steps if the police officers had taken just a few fruits from him and one of them had slightly twisted his mouth in such a way that the fruit seller could have interpreted this as a supportive smile. Tiny changes at the beginning of the chain can lead to completely different results in the end.

The American scientist and meteorologist Edward Lorenz, in a lecture to the "American Association for the Advancement of Science" in 1972, made the comparison for the first time that the flapping of a butterfly‘s wings in the Brazilian jungle could provoke a tornado in Texas (Lorenz 1972). This is an abbreviation of quite complex chains of causes that is immediately comprehensible to natural scientists but sounds somehow unserious to most other people.

Example

Therefore, imagine that on the TV show Domino -Day (that was the one where millions of people watched dominoes that had been painstakingly built up over hours fall over so that the TV station could get a new entry in the Guinness Book of Records at the end) there were two rows of dominoes set up in parallel, each triggering different reactions.

The first row continues in the game and triggers the typical domino effects: In the end, many pretty pictures were created, the audience was entertained great and the world record for the most dominoes knocked over was broken (once again).

The second row, however, runs towards a small block that serves as a brake for a six-ton rock ball. This begins to roll down a ramp, getting faster and faster and ends up running unstoppably towards the spotlights, cameras and the control room …

Depending on which row is triggered, this TV show would have a completely different ending—the differences could hardly be greater. And now we come to the butterfly in question, because both rows are triggered by a single, feather-light first domino, whose path can be altered by even the slightest breath of air. And while this first domino moves towards the two rows, a butterfly flies past it … ◀

So a minimal deviation of the initial conditions causes completely different results. Rounding in the fifth place after the decimal point of the initial data results in completely different pictures for the next day in the weather forecast. And now imagine that you want to derive a vision of the future for your industry from the past—with all the interactions that make up a market …

That's what Edward Lorenz meant by the butterfly in Brazil. But I find my version more entertaining—especially when I had to watch this TV show for hours again for my mother's sake.

- We basically have to come to terms with chaos in all parts of our lives. You'd better not try to escape it by small-scale planning for the future. Your planning will in no way be improved by this.

2.6 Bias 6: Physical Laws

As you can see, there are a multitude of physical reasons why it is very difficult to see into the future. A gentleman by the name of Werner Heisenberg postulated another physical difficulty almost 90 years ago, which since then can also be seen in all other fields, such as economics.

Example

Do you have children? In our home, there was a certain shelf in the kitchen where sweets were stored—including chocolate. Imagine that you, as a parent, take a look up there and find the shelf ransacked, the chocolate stash miraculously melted away. Then you know exactly *what* happened there, but you don't know *when* your children looted the shelf.

On the other hand, your kids may be so suspiciously quiet in the kitchen. You know that dead silence, right? Then you realize that there is some nonsense going on there right now, but you don't know exactly what.

After all, if you want to know both the "what" and the "when", then you have to go into the kitchen and watch your children do it. But since your children are not stupid, then of course, nothing will happen—you have already changed the situation yourself just by observing. This is—in a figurative sense and a nutshell—the Heisenberg uncertainty principle. The more precise you want to look at one aspect—for example, the "when"—the less precise another aspect will have to be. ◀

What exactly does this mean for forecasting the future? Well, it simply means that you can only make limited detailed statements about the future. Think of your daily forecast in the 24-hour self-experiment: You may be able to say with a certain probability that a regularly scheduled meeting will also take place tomorrow—but you will not be able to say exactly when this meeting will end. Or take an everyday business forecast:

Example

Sales forecast

Let's assume you sell TV sets, the market is rather stable overall and none of your competitors is planning to launch an unusual promotion or a radical new development. Then, assuming you have good planning tools, you will probably be able to plan a *month-*

by-month volume sale that can be fairly accurate as a statistical average across all models. However, due to the broad distribution, you cannot possibly plan which dealer will take exactly which share of the quantities.

On the other hand, you know your distribution well and know which dealer is particularly strong in which product category or price class. You can therefore predict *annual sales* for individual dealers or dealer groups—perhaps even with model accuracy. However, you will be absolutely shipwrecked if you want to determine sales location (=dealer) and sales time (=month) exactly at the same time. ◄

In physics, this limitation of accuracy is called *Heisenberg's uncertainty principle,* which refers to the pure observation of processes in the present. But the above example makes it clear that even future developments of interdependent variables cannot be planned with arbitrary accuracy.

▶ The more accurately you try to determine one factor, the greater the inaccuracies of the other factors will be.

2.7 Bias 7: Experts

A few years ago, after an attack, there was once again a special news show on tv, to which a serious-looking man was added who, according to the title, was a "terrorism expert". The presenter read off her contributions from the usual cards prepared by the editors, so she asked unconcernedly: "After this attack—should we expect more similar attacks in other cities in near future?" I felt sorry for the interviewee. How was the poor man supposed to know? Unless, perhaps, he had acquired his expert status by playing cards with potential terrorists every Thursday night. But that was not likely to happen.

But instead of refusing such a stupid question, the "expert" kept his composure and started answering pseudo-seriously in the style of a university professor. You won't be surprised to learn that he did not have anything relevant to say. After all, whether terrorists or other maniacs would now repeat this exact attack in other cities, he could not possibly know. And to answer the question of whether there would be a danger of further attacks somewhere in the world in the future, one would not need experts, but only common sense. But it would have been far less interesting for the viewers if the presenter had simply answered this question herself.

You see here the role that experts can only play: They can try to use their knowledge to identify the context and explain it to us non-knowers. Provided that they avoid—as far as feasible—the error of retrospective logic already discussed, this may help us to be able to evaluate assessments for the future. But they cannot make forecasts themselves any better than other people: Experts are experts for the current state, not for the future.

Incidentally, this was also the result of a long-term study conducted over almost 20 years by the US scientist Philip Tetlock, for which he obtained detailed predictions from 250 recognised political experts. The result was so devastating that it circulated in the scientific community, but also in the New York Times (Stevens 2012) and the Wall Street Journal (Kueppers 2001) in the form of a joke: according to this, the average expert would be about as accurate with his predictions as a chimpanzee throwing darts at a dartboard while blindfolded.

In his later book *Superforecasting* on prediction techniques, Tetlock attempts a bit of honorific redemption and himself marginally qualifies this judgment: experts showed good results on questions of the near future. Even with predictions that were only three to 5 years in the future, however, the experts had arrived at darts-throwing chimpanzees (Tetlock 2017).

Of course, this judgement does not only apply to political forecasts: We have already laughed heartily about the lack of wealth of investment bankers—religious fanatics have been predicting the end of the world for the last 4000 years just as vainly as technical experts have been predicting technological development. As proxy examples, consider quotes from Thomas Watson (Chairman of IBM, 1943: "… there may be a need in the world for about five computers …"), Bill Gates (Microsoft, 1993: "… the Internet, it's just hype …"), or Steve Balmer (Microsoft, 2007: "The iPhone has no chance of gaining significant market share) …" (Dunn 2016).

Experts, as the scientifically flawlessly evaluated study by Philip Tetlock shows, are subject to the same bias, i.e., the same systematic errors in the assessment of future developments, as any other person. And many forecasts, especially when it comes to longer-term forecasts (from 3 to 5 years!), could have been obtained much cheaper, namely already for a Euro coin: With that, predictions—with equal probability—can be made by simply flipping the coin upside down.

2.8 Bias 8: Extrapolations

Experts, as we have just seen, are—if they are serious—primarily experts for the present. They understand conceivable contexts and if they use this experience to conclude about a possible future, they only can predict events that will come by pure chance. It is again the non-calculable coincidence that speaks against a meaningful prediction.

Example

In an experiment cited by Philip Tetlock (Tetlock 2017, p. 40), the scientists Edwards and Estel are said to have constructed a T-shaped corridor and placed rats in it. On each of the two upper sides of the corridor was a food flap, which was opened purely at random—but in such a way that, in total, one side opened in 40% of the trials, while the other opened 60% of the time. After a short time, the rats had developed a feeling for the probabilities—at least if we assumed that rats are not capable of counting—and from then on simply sat dutifully in front of the 60 percent door. A group of students, presented with the same set-up, began an elaborate search (!) for a pattern in the opening frequency and ideally calculated it—except that there was no pattern at all. As a result, the intellectually very far ahead students typed the result—the future—significantly worse than the rats. ◀

Shouldn't that be a hint for dealing with expert predictions? Well, you may counter that your sales department's plan for next year's sales is, after all, also based on past values and will nevertheless occur with acceptable deviations. However, this is not in itself a contradiction. A prediction is a view into the future, while the term forecast is mainly used based on number crunching adding known disturbing factors (seasonality, weather, etc.). After all, the prediction is what we have to deal with for your future market.

In this respect, your sales planning is a forecast that can function for up to 1 or 2 years, depending on the market situation—this corresponds exactly to the statement that Tetlock has also identified as a possible hit period for the political experts. However, the further away you get from today, the less accurate your planning becomes. In the area of road construction machinery, product-specific planning may still make sense up to the third year; in the area of short-lived household electronics, the end of usefulness is sometimes reached after 6 months.

The Great Horse Manure Crisis of 1894

At the end of the nineteenth century, population numbers and the associated traffic in the world's major cities grew so rapidly that city planners began to have real concerns: Some 50,000 horses pulled carriages, carts and horse-drawn buses in London alone, leaving behind up to 10L of urine and up to 20kg of excrement per horse per day, which was by no means disposed of carefully. Population growth was extrapolated, and an article in the London Times in 1894 concluded that if development continued as it had with the population explosion and the horses it required, the city would be buried under nearly three meters of horse manure 50 years later—in 1940s (Johnson 2015). It was such a horrific scenario that it became the main topic in the first global urban planning conference, planned for ten days in 1898in New York. After just three days of brainstorming, participants left the ten-day conference frustrated and without a solution. This was brought about in 1912 by a black swan in the form of the automobile …

The scenario Great Horse Manure Crisis sounds very bizarre to our ears, but it is by no means a joke—people were discussing such possibilities 120 years ago. Does that seem completely exaggerated to you? But it is a reality.

Such misjudgements have been commonplace at all times and, let us be sure, will continue to be so today and in the future: Today, for example, we discuss with great energy the effects of the expected global warming and, depending on one's point of view, are quite sure that sea levels may rise by several meters. But think back, if you remember—to the 1970s. At that time, the same profession of meteorologists was engaged in a very similar looking battle for the front page of the newspapers with the theme "next ice age":

The Next Ice Age

A little look at climate coverage in the daily press in the 70s:

- "American journalists described the cold in the east of the country as a 'foretaste of the next ice age'. Frost down to minus 50 degrees and snow up to six metres high transformed large parts of the United States into a polar landscape.... (Frankfurter Allgemeine Zeitung, 25.02.1977)" (Kulke 2009)

- "Is a new ice age looming? Nigel Calder (former editor of the respected British New Scientist) thinks this is likely and recently published a book with current research results to prove it. (Süddeutsche Zeitung, 10.04.1975)" (Kulke 2009)
- "For the past decade, temperatures have been falling. Yet many meteorologists fear that there may be a 'point of no return' from which polluted air will inevitably and inexorably affect the climate. The winter of 1968/69 brought ice cover to the North Atlantic that had not been seen for nearly sixty years. A lot of ice reflects a lot of solar radiation back out into space and consumes a lot of heat to melt. (Hamburger Abendblatt, 21.03.1970)" (Kulke 2009).

These misconceptions are just 40 years old and somehow sound alien, don't they? So why are we so sure that we are on a more realistic path with our current assessment of the future than our colleagues in the ice age faction or the horse manure skeptics?

Pure extrapolation is therefore in no way suitable for assessing the future. Those who nevertheless take this route run the risk of being drastically caught up with reality. Like the Christmas geese, for example, who have to discover this again and again in a particularly painful way: First comes a cheerful human face every morning for 210 days in a row, opening the barn door and the way to the green meadow, providing food in large quantities, offering protection from foxes and other vermin, and bringing everyone back into sleep in the evening unharmed. What a loving treatment—surely that's 30 weeks of pure wellness. If some geese would take these results—statistically quite correct—and extrapolate the development using an Excel trend function, they could conclude that their wonderful life would stay like this forever. But then there is the visit of the butcher in the 31st week …

And to prevent you running into the same trap, here's an older but very timely quote on "extrapolating from the past to the future" (Butler 2012):

> When anyone asks me how I can best describe my experience in nearly forty years at sea, I merely say, uneventful. Of course, there have been winter gales, and storms and fog and the like. But in all my experience, I have never been in an accident… or any sort worth speaking about. I have seen but one vessel in distress in all my years at sea. I never saw a wreck and never have been wrecked nor was I ever in any predicament that threatened to end in disaster of any sort.
>
> (E. J. Smith 1907, later captain of the RMS Titanic)

References

Butler DA (2012) Unsinkable: the full story of the RMS titanic, kindle. Da Capo Press, Cambridge

Deutscher Bundestag (2012) Bericht zur Risikoanalyse im Bevölkerungsschutz 2012. https://dipbt.bundestag.de/dip21/btd/17/120/1712051.pdf. Zugegriffen: 15. Mai 2020

Dobelli R (2011) Die Kunst des klaren Denkens–52 Denkfehler, die Sie besser anderen überlassen. Hanser, München

Dunn M (2016) Here are 20 of the worst predictions ever made about the future of tech. https://www.news.com.au/technology/gadgets/here-are-20-of-the-worst-predictions-ever-made-about-the-future-of-tech/news-story/2300ac1ffb8a3ba18ce3219636700937. Zugegriffen: 20. Mai 2020

Hilbig H (2013) Marketing ist eine Wissenschaft … Springer Gabler, Wiesbaden

Jischa MF (2009) Gedanken zur Wahrnehmung der Zukunft. In: Popp R, Schüll E (Hrsg) Zukunftsforschung und Zukunftsgestaltung. Zukunft und Forschung. Springer, Berlin, S 37

Kueppers A (2001) Blindfolded monkey beats humans with stock picks. https://www.wsj.com/articles/SB991681622136214659. Zugegriffen: 18. Mai 2020

Johnson B (2015) The great horse manure crisis of 1894. https://www.historic-uk.com/HistoryUK/HistoryofBritain/Great-Horse-Manure-Crisis-of-1894/. Zugegriffen: 20. Mai 2020

Kulke U (2009) Als uns vor 30 Jahren eine neue Eiszeit drohte. https://www.welt.de/wissenschaft/umwelt/article5489379/Als-uns-vor-30-Jahren-eine-neue-Eiszeit-drohte.html. Zugegriffen: 20. Mai 2020

Lorenz E (1972) Predictability: Does the flap of a butterfly's wings in Brazil set of a tornado in Texas? https://eaps4.mit.edu/research/Lorenz/Butterfly_1972.pdf. Zugegriffen: 19. Mai 2020

Spiegel Online (2017) Turnier-Neuling gewinnt 8,1 Millionen Dollar. https://www.spiegel.de/panorama/world-series-of-poker-scott-blumstein-gewinnt-8-1-millionen-dollar-a-1159294.html. Zugegriffen: 18. Mai 2020

Stevens J (2012) Political scientists are lousy forecasters. https://www.nytimes.com/2012/06/24/opinion/sunday/political-scientists-are-lousy-forecasters.html. Zugegriffen: 18. Mai 2020

Taleb NN (2014) Der schwarze Schwan–Die Macht höchst unwahrscheinlicher Ereignisse. DTV, München

Tetlock PE (2017) Expert political judgment: how good is it? How can we know? Princeton University Press, Princeton

Tetlock PE, Gardner D (2016) Superforecasting–Die Kunst der richtigen Prognose. Fischer, Frankfurt a. M

Learning from the Mistakes and Successes of Others

3

Abstract

Based on ten analyzed case studies, examples of successful and less successful strategies for the future are presented. In addition to the thinking errors listed in Chap. 2, other strategic mistakes are presented, some of them tragic, which have driven companies to ruin. Equally, however, there are success stories that tell of ingenious moves and the luck of the brave. The examples include the stories of well-known current brands such as Ikea, Shell, Casio or the Rügenwalder Mühle as well as companies whose shine has now faded such as Kodak, Time/system or Olympia, and serve to identify the systematic nature of successful future management.

On the following pages, I would like to show, somewhat abbreviated, a few examples of companies that have prepared for the future in very different ways—and therefore with very different degrees of success. I have deliberately focused these examples on well-known brands and less on the SME factor. The reason for this is that you can easily research these cases yourself on the Internet if you find my presentation here too brief. This is an advantage that is no longer possible with one or the other less successful medium-sized companies. For your fact check, you will find links and sources for each case study in Sect. 8.4.

We start with the less beautiful examples, from which one can learn a lot, however—and then end with some successful companies. Since everyone is a good general after the war—and I don't want to exclude myself at all—for each example there is a short assessment of what probably were the success or failure factors.

H. Hilbig, *Shaping the Future of Your Business*,
https://doi.org/10.1007/978-3-658-35349-0_3

This will lead us to the later chapters (see Sects. 3.4 to 4.6), where we will deal with how to combine the factors found into a practicable concept and implement it with the available resources even of medium-sized companies.

3.1 Kodak: A Market Does Not Belong to any Company

In the 1990s the company had 180,000 employees under contract worldwide and made multiple profits on virtually every photo taken on the planet. It had an 80% market share in photographic papers and a similarly lucky hand in films and laboratories. We are talking about the Eastman Kodak Corporation, a company that dominated the photographic industry that absolutely nothing happened without Kodak‘s “approval”. At the big photo fairs in the USA and Germany, the company always insisted on having its exclusive hall so that it could present itself appropriately. In short: Kodak was doing extremely well and felt unassailable.

In the year of the (first) catastrophe—2012—in which the group had to file for bankruptcy and place itself under the protection of Chap. 11 of the US Bankruptcy Code, the company had assets of over five billion US dollars—but unfortunately also over seven billion US dollars in liabilities. How could it have come to this? After all, Kodak was an entrepreneurial institution—similar to Facebook, Google or Amazon today. And like these companies, the photo giant was proactive, constantly on the lookout for new, innovative areas of business and quite unconventional in its approach: in 2007, for example, a research reactor containing 1.5 kg of weapons-grade uranium was discovered in the basement of the headquarters in Rochester (USA) (WeltN24, 16.05.2012). The company had wanted to use it to test the durability of photos.

Part of that search included hiring engineer Steven J. Sasson, only 24 years old, in 1973, whose very first task was to find a useful application for one of the first image sensors available. So Sasson began experimenting in a small lab in Rochester and created something that he presented to his superiors in 1975: an ugly, light blue box with a Super 8 lens from the old parts store and an audio cassette hanging open on the right side. On this cassette, he stored in digital form the image captured by the sensor and then played it back via a conventional television set (Fig. 3.1).

The whole thing was, measured by our today’s standard, not that impressive: A black and white picture with 10,000 pixels (your smartphone doesn’t make it under 20 million!), which was finally saved on tape after almost half a minute. But: It was de facto the first digital camera.

What happened next is something I have experienced time and again in a different form with successful companies: Steven Sasson was not allowed to publish his

Fig. 3.1 The first digital camera from 1975. (Source: Associated Press/dpa Picture-Alliance GmbH)

invention. "I wasn't allowed to say a word about it," he later said in an interview with Der Spiegel. The official reason given for sending him back to the basement, was that they did not think, anyone would even want to look at his pictures on a TV screen. But if it was just about the poor business prospects of an unpromising technology, why the total secrecy?

His superiors feared that this new technology would cut into the company's film profits. Kodak's entire financial success, after all, had been based on making and selling consumables for nearly a hundred years. So protecting its ongoing business was the real motive. Why would they want to compete with themselves? And because of the company's size and dominant position in the photographic market, they were convinced that they could control developments in their interests in such a way that their profitability would not be diminished.

A fatal miscalculation, as it later turned out. Kodak's analysts had foreseen the digital transformation of the market early on in the mid-1990s—Sasson's invention was merely the translation into practical products, so to speak. But those responsible at Kodak had no interest in changes happening in a future 20 years away:

"When you're talking to a bunch of corporate guys about 18 to 20 years in the future when none of those guys will still be in the company, they do not get too excited about it," Sasson said in a New York Times interview (Estrin 2015) later. For these managers, short-term sales success and perhaps their bonuses took precedence over long-term strategic decisions. They allowed Sasson to continue, however, and in 1978 he applied for a patent for his invention under US4131919A. He later went on to work on solutions that could be used to convert high-end SLR cameras to digital image capture. But Kodak completely overslept the lucrative camera hardware market. Even when Casio, a pure electronics company without any photographic background, presented the first marketable digital camera for consumers at the end of 1994 with the QV-10—and even irritated all Japanese camera manufacturers—they continued sleeping in Rochester. By the time they finally began to take this development seriously, it was already too late: the analogue photo market had already taken a nosedive by the end of the 1990s, and the company's digital cameras, which Kodak had finally manufactured in the Far East, were crude boxes compared to the already more advanced models of the Japanese competition, and by that simply no longer met consumer demands in terms of technology and design. Kodak had not made use of its 20-year head start.

The company tried to turn the wheel one last time by demanding license fees from every camera manufacturer for the use of the patent from 1996 onwards. But even that was unsuccessful: with the original invention of the digital camera by Steven Sasson, Kodak had been so far ahead of the market that the mass market only took off when the original patent had already expired in 1998. Sometimes you may be (too) far ahead of your time.

In 2012, Eastman Kodak Company filed for bankruptcy under Chap. 11 of the U.S. Bankruptcy Code. Today, the remnants of the company still consist of individual successor organizations with different business areas and shareholders, which still employ 7000 people worldwide. In nowadays it takes time to find a Kodak stand at the remaining photo fairs in the meantime …

Kodak: The Three Most Important Mistakes

- Kodak overestimated its influence on the development of the photographic market.
- competing offers were rejected rather than addressed.
- Kodak's main focus in competitive intelligence was on direct competition, not on sideline attacks.

3.2 Olympia: Visions of the Future without Imagination

The next company to which we turn our attention has a similar history to Kodak—and was quite similarly successful in its field. It was founded in 1903 under the name Union Schreibmaschinen-Gesellschaft m.b.H. in Germany as a subsidiary of AEG and at its peak employed more than 20,000 people—in addition to the subcontracting companies that were not counted. We are talking about Olympia—or more precisely Olympia Büromaschinenwerke AG. The group expanded so much during the post-war years that at its peak it ranked with IBM (USA) and Olivetti (Italy) among the three largest office machine factories in the world. Like Kodak, Olympia was keen to demonstrate this greatness: In the newly opened Hall 1 (the "Cebit Hall") of the Hanover Fair in 1970, Olympia was the largest exhibitor.

Further parallels to Kodak can also be found in the preparation for the future: Olympia had been founded as a typewriter manufacturer and had become successful, but it was constantly on the lookout for further business fields. During the Second World War, the company built the Enigma, the legendary cipher machine of the German Reich—the star of many Hollywood movies—but of course, no mass business could be built on it. Especially since the whole thing was so secret that nobody noticed. Okay, except for the US forces, perhaps, who unceremoniously dismantled the manufacturing plant in Erfurt in April 1945.

In the search for promising future markets, Olympia, therefore, entered into the construction of data acquisition and calculating machines, bought corresponding plants or cooperated, for example, with the Japanese company Matsushita—the predecessor of today's electronics group Panasonic.

Olympia continuously expanded its product range to include products that fitted in with the brand core "office machines" in the broadest sense, but without being able to build up deep expertise there itself. The calculating machines, for example, were all based on the so-called Nixie tubes, which some of you may still remember from old films or the museum: The displays consisted of glowing orange digits from 0 to 9, mounted one behind the other in a light bulb-like construction, and no doubt consumed an unspeakably large amount of electricity. The products were heavy, expensive, blew fuses—and just weren't competitive in any way with modern transistor-based calculators from Japanese companies.

Interestingly, however, Olympia's management hardly invested any energy in taking its core business, typewriters, into the next millennium. It is true that the typewriters of the 1970s became more and more powerful models with writing memory and displays or even with the connection to external data media ("for an almost unlimited writing volume"—according to Olympia's advertising), and with the product *Olytext 20* the company even brought a product onto the market in 1986 that was the spitting image of IBMs personal computer of 1981. But even *Olytext* was just a further developed typewriter. The basic error in thinking was that the management simply could not imagine a separation of capturing, storing and printing texts in the workflow of an office and therefore kept thinking about "optimised typewriters".

And yet such approaches did exist within the Group. Only 25 km from the former Wilhelmshaven site, on the other side of the Jade Bay, there is now a company in Varel (Microplex Printware AG) that builds on technologies originally developed at Olympia. Today, industrial printers are successfully built there that can be integrated into any IT system without any effort.

The Olympia management at the time, however, had no sense for such developments. The former market dominance and the central importance that typewriters still represented for the company led to tunnel vision—a phenomenon that can be observed time and again, especially among market leaders. And so, even in the 1980s, Olympia continued to focus on ever more perfect automatic typewriters, while computers with word processing programs made their way into offices and private households.

Olympia—like its parent companies AEG and Daimler—was caught up with the future—or rather, caught cold.

Olympia: The Three Most Important Mistakes

- Olympia was also subject to the belief that, as one of the global market leaders, it could control the development of the market itself.
- Like Kodak, there was a lack of critical engagement with competing technologies emerging in parallel.
- When these then became relevant to the market, the company did not react flexibly enough to recognise the opportunities in the new technologies.

3.3 Swissair: Overestimating its Position

I was told the following story almost 20 years ago by a management consultant whose employer was involved in the case described and who experienced this part of the story himself.

The early 1990s saw a further stage in the liberalisation of air transport. Over the years, more and more market-based elements were added to the formerly predominantly state-regulated matter of flying, such as the liberalisation of prices in the course of the third liberalisation package of 1992. As a result, airlines suddenly had to assert themselves in a free market—a completely new market situation: there were no longer any competition-free flight connections or minimum margins guaranteed by price agreements. The previously so satisfactory business figures of the airlines threatened to turn into a friendly bright red. Airlines formed alliances in order to be able to make better offers together. In Europe, three main clusters formed around the major airlines of Germany (Lufthansa), France (Air France) and Great Britain (British Airways). For all other smaller European airlines, the question was whether to join one of these three clusters or to look for alternative strategies. One airline was particularly affected by this: Swissair.

At the beginning of the 1990s, Swissair was an absolute flagship airline, carrying significantly more passengers than the Swiss airline market had to offer. One of the reasons for this: Swissair was considered by frequent flyers to be one of the best airlines in the world with outstanding service, qualitatively unbeatable catering onboard, extremely comfortable seats (by the standards of the time) and a very well-developed route network. Frequent flyers who were allowed to select the airline to travel with had chosen Swissair.

In 1989, long before the formation of the major alliances, Swissair was the first company to establish the Global Excellence Alliance with the US airline Delta and Singapore Airlines, which was now, however, in danger of failing in the mid-1990s. To keep Delta in line, Swissair had to capture ever-larger market shares in the European air business and tried to achieve this, first through new cooperations and later through sometimes very dubious holdings in a wide variety of airlines. Nevertheless, Delta left the alliance with Swissair at the end of the 1990s and turned to Air France, with which it then formed the SkyTeam alliance. The Swiss company was left with a huge mountain of debt and very shaky holdings in airlines, some of which were struggling financially. The flagship company had almost abruptly become a restructuring case, and the CEO at the time was therefore trying to save money wherever possible.

In this situation, two facts came to the board's attention that had a significant influence on further proceedings. Firstly, it was loudly propagated within the Group that the cost structure of the second brand Crossair would be considerably more favourable than that of the parent company Swissair. Secondly, this seemed to be confirmed by benchmarking with the northern competitor Lufthansa. The Germans also flew much more cheaply than the Swiss, which seemed to be essentially due to a leaner personnel structure: The German airline flew with considerably fewer personnel per 1000 passengers than the Swiss' white Cross.

As a result, a drastic cost-cutting program was launched: 500 million Swiss francs were to be saved within 2 years, 1200 jobs were to be cut and the route network thinned out. Tragic decisions that hit the main target group of frequent flyers to the core, because now the best airline in the world suddenly became a budget airline: The much praised cuisine above the clouds disappeared, the number of flight attendants per flight was reduced and Swissair was already no longer the first choice of frequent flyers because it thinned out the flight schedule so that certain routes were no longer offered at all.

The end of the story is quickly told: The drastic, ever-growing over-indebtedness could no longer be managed in the early 2000s, the company flew into bankruptcy at the end of 2001, and the last plane took off on April 1, 2002. A new company, Swiss, was then founded from the remains of the once-proud airline.

Unlike the previous two examples, there were a variety of reasons and wrong decisions for the ultimate failure of Swissair. Particularly tragic, however, is the part concerning the cost-cutting measures that were implemented. Because here, the airline's managers worked with false benchmarks: The figures of the subsidiary Crossair were correct in the group's own controlling but concealed the fact that Crossair was able to use several services as parts of the group without having to explicitly show them in its costs per passenger.

And the benchmark with the Germans? Was simply wrong. The values for the KPI "number of employees per 1000 passengers" were compared—except that at Lufthansa this figure was defined as the number of flying personnel per 1000 passengers, whereas at Swissair it was understood to be the total number of all employees per 1000 passengers—including the personnel on the ground.

Swissair: The Three Most Important Mistakes

Strictly speaking, the same mistake was made three times in a row at Swissair: a me-too strategy was pursued by copying the strategies of other, much larger airlines without taking into account the airline's strengths and weaknesses:

- In choosing a strategy for the future, management had opted for the role of junior partner to Delta in preparation for the expected liberalisation of the market, although this partnership appears to have been shaky from the outset. This forcibly drove the small but highly successful Swissair into an unhealthy growth strategy.
- After the cooperation with Delta had collapsed, the airline relied on a concept that was exemplified by the three major European airlines and founded its alliance.
- As the edifice began to totter, management once again sought a solution in copying the strategy of others, using (false) benchmarks to compare and control their offerings.

3.4 Daimler/AEG/Olympia: Failing to Recognize Opportunities

A situation that will certainly sound familiar to the parents among you: Your child comes home in a rage and declares with a determined expression: "I can't go there anymore—that's where the big kids are now." With that, it has opened up to its parents that there was once again the war of the half meters on some playground. Sometimes it was "the tall ones", sometimes it was the "stupid cow" next door. In any case, the little one did not feel like going to that one playground anymore. What is the right reaction to this?

If we exclude the variant, that you solve your child's problem by talking to the "tall ones" directly, then the only thing left to do is to talk to the child about possible alternatives. Alternative behaviors, alternative friends, or even alternative times to use the playground. Under no circumstances will any parent simply accept the child's withdrawal not to go there any longer: A child who withdraws from playgrounds without coming up with ideas for alternatives will become quite lonely over time. After all, there won't be so many playgrounds around its home. But if we as adults reject such simple withdrawals from our children, shouldn't this also apply to the big ones, like brands and enterprises, too?

Let's take another look back at the German typewriter market leader Olympia. The direct wrong decision was of course Olympia itself, whose management could not think and act outside the learned tunnel and thus simply missed the transition from a major office machine supplier to an office electronics supplier. But there was a second, deeper level to the story: the parent companies (shouldn't we rather speak of mother and grandmother?) AEG and Daimler also missed their chance. Because while the Olympia management was only caught in tunnel vision, the AEG and Daimler managers missed out on being one of the first companies to play a massive role in the brave new electronic world of office communications, in which the Olympia subsidiary at least already had a good foot in the door. In 1991, the weekly newspaper "Die Zeit" wrote in an interview with the then chairman of the board of the Daimler empire (Eglau 1991): "At least at AEG, Edzard Reuter by no means absolves himself of his misjudgements. Thus, as he freely admitted, he 'regretted afterward' having declared office communications as a core business area as late as 1988." He had regretted having regarded office communications as a core business? In which universe did the man live—and with him the whole Daimler management?

At the time of the interview in 1991, the IBM PC had already been on the market for 10 years. How big the topic of office communications would be one day, became apparent on March 12, 1986 at the latest, when the first independent computer show CeBit was held on the grounds of Hannover Messe AG, outgrown from the information technology section of the "old" Hannover Messe. Oh yes, and almost exactly 2 months before the interview, on August 6, 1991, Tim Berners-Lee (Wikipedia 2017) published the basic features of the Internet as we know it today and made it usable.

Admittedly, if you had to enter the great new playgrounds of the information age with nixie tubes and type-lever typewriters, you could only lose. But what opportunities did Daimler miss when it decided for itself and its subsidiary AEG to retreat without alternative (and thus to death for its granddaughter Olympia)?

Daimler/AEG/Olympia: The Three Most Important Mistakes

- Because of the dependencies, the "withdrawal from office communications" was a typical corporate error. Those who should have known better had little influence on the decision. And those who decided had no overview of the opportunities of the new market.
- In addition, it appears that neither Daimler nor its subsidiaries AEG and Olympia had processes in place to develop viable scenarios for the future. They simply could not imagine that office communications would become one of the transformative issues of the coming century.
- At the critical time for Olympia, the wrong group of corporate managers was at the helm in all three groups. Where expansion should have taken place, the focus was instead on cost reduction.

3.5 Polaroid et al.: You cannot Win by Retreating

A more recent example of a company that has completely lost its market significance through withdrawal is the US company Polaroid, which enjoyed great success with instant pictures in the 1970s and 1980s, and in 1985 even successfully brought the photo giant Kodak to its knees in court, which had tried to sell its instant picture system. The market became difficult for Polaroid in the mid-1990s, when, what seemed to be the only product advantage—the instant availability of the image—was now covered by digital cameras of much better quality. Polaroid withdrew further and further in many steps. First, the development of new products in the consumer market was discontinued, then the hitherto highly profitable "passport photo photography"division—and with the increasing digitalization of professional photography, the chapter of Polaroid proofs in the photo studio also ended: Polaroid filed for bankruptcy for the first time in 2001.

Incidentally, instant photography itself is by no means as dead as one might think: While today's Polaroid owners have sworn off the technique altogether, instead of sticking the brand on all manner of third-party merchandise, former competitor Fujifilm is enjoying an unprecedented run on instant cameras whose images are even smaller than what Polaroid used to offer. Given the infinitely shared internet, the desire for ephemera seems to have created new markets …

Withdrawal from the business as the only strategic approach? Such an approach is more common than one might think. We will explore the reasons for this in Sect. 4.6 ("Just among us: Are you the right manager for the job?").

However, such an approach makes absolutely no sense if all competitors in a market are committed to the same idea. This was the case a few years ago in the market for digital cameras. In Table 3.1 you will find a small compilation of then current news. These are the quotes from some press releases of the most important Asian suppliers from the last few years.

Table 3.1 Development of a "sector strategy

Date	Manufacturer	Quote press releases
May 14, 2012	Samsung	The Korean manufacturer plans to produce more system cameras instead of digital compacts at its largest Chinese manufacturing facility in the future (Photoscala 2012)
June 8, 2012	Olympus	In the imaging sector, the company intends to focus on mirrorless and ambitious compact cameras (Maschke 2012).
June 17, 2015	Casio	Casio abandons the camera market in Europe (Buttlar 2015)
November 21, 2015	Samsung	Exit from the camera business (Kuhn 2015)
July 29, 2016	Fujifilm	Fuji wants to counter this (loss of sales) in the future with an even stronger focus on high-quality (and thus high-priced) products (Photoscala 2016a).
November 8, 2016	Nikon	Nikon wants to focus on high-priced products that promise decent profits. With this, the company is likely to say goodbye to the compact camera business (Photoscala 2016b).
February 13, 2017	Nikon	Nikon today officially announced the end of its premium DL-series compact cameras (Photoscala 2017a)
February 27, 2017	Nikon	Nikon to focus on profitable system cameras (Photoscala 2017b)
April 13, 2017	Ricoh	Ricoh explains that the company will focus on "high added value products" .... With this, Ricoh only clarifies what has long been obvious: the company no longer offers classic compact cameras (Photoscala 2017c).

Until 2010, the global market for digital cameras had grown a good bit every year. When, from 2011 onwards, there were increasing signs that such growth could no longer be relied upon, the strategists at the company's Asian headquarters felt that a gradual withdrawal from the small compact camera business was the only effective way to save the profit situation. This seemed to be a good approach: if they gave up the part of the market[1] that accounted for 90% of the market in terms of volume but only generated losses in terms of earnings, then this had to contribute to an increase in profits, didn't it?

Probably not. For one thing, the more profitable high-end market also shrank drastically, so that this seemingly tastier cake per se became smaller and smaller. On the other hand, a market strategy that only focuses on a small, profitable segment in the future simply cannot work if all competitors follow the same strategy. And that all competitors were pursuing the same strategy was already evident from the press releases published—see Table 3.1. Why didn't the strategists at the Asian company headquarters notice this?

Polaroid: The Three Most Important Mistakes

Certainly, in each of these case studies there were and still are a large number of strategic mistakes that led to the unpleasant results of the companies and industries under consideration. But the most decisive—and thus for once the only one named here—failure factor is this: a retreat without developing alternatives is not a strategy for the future!

By the way: How one can deal with difficulties in a completely different way than the companies mentioned can be seen in a small start-up that repeatedly faced situations threatening its existence, especially in its early days: IKEA.

3.6 Ikea: Identifying Opportunities in Challenges

Software companies suffer from the fact that unplanned behaviour can quickly occur in the program code—after all, it is difficult to completely test all processes of a complex program, possibly even on different operating systems and their numerous versions. As a kind of proactive excuse with a smile, software developers ex-

[1] Until around 2010, compact cameras accounted for 85 to 90% of the total market in terms of volume, depending on the region (CIPA).

plain such misbehaviour of their software as part of the plan: Unplanned reaction are no bugs, but an intended feature. It's not a bug, it's a feature—that's the perfect description of the following example:

Ingvar Kamprad was a young entrepreneur who faced merciless competition and price war shortly after founding his company. Using the mail-order sales method, which was still unusual in his industry at the time, he was able to offer products at significantly lower prices than his stationary competitors. Since they were unable to follow due to the basic costs caused by operating the retail stores, they tried to take advantage of their market position by cutting the young entrepreneur off from the flow of goods. A situation in which many other founders might have given up and withdrawn from this market (see Sect. 2.6). Not so Ingvar, whose fighting spirit now seemed all the more fired up: In a night-and-night operation, he sought out producers who could manufacture and supply his own products for him. This turned out to be a brilliant move, because it not only allowed him to circumvent the boycott measures of his competitors but also gave him complete control over the design of his products. The entrepreneur was Ingvar Kamprad—and his company was called Ikea from the very beginning (Fig. 3.2).

Fig. 3.2 The first warehouse of the small start-up. (Courtesy of © Ikea Deutschland GmbH & Co KG [2017]. All Rights Reserved)

However, this strategic move also had a disadvantage, because now Ingvar no longer sold well-known brand products, but his own goods, which, moreover, no customer could see beforehand. Ingvar's customers had to order "blindly", so to speak, only on the word of the small company.

Yes, I know, that's nothing special in the age of e-commerce anymore. But back in Ingvar's day, it was. And so it was the turn of the unfair competitors, who began to spread the word that Ingvar's goods were inferior products. So the young entrepreneur was once again faced with a choice: retreat or … attack!

Quality had always been important to him—but now he had to prove that quality to his potential customers. Ingvar opened a showroom where interested parties could view and order all his products. Like his competitors, he now also had a stationary branch, but on completely different terms: Instead of using a few samples to sell the goods in a consultation-intensive manner, Ingvar's customers could view all the products in the showroom themselves, check them out and then also order them. 2:0 for the newcomer.

The next problem was homemade—at least that's the official legend: The concept of own products, showrooms and high quality at low prices worked so well that the opening of the first showroom in the capital almost led to a traffic collapse. In historical pictures, you can see long lines of shoppers outside the building's gates, against which even iPhone queues look rather tired. And inside, things continued: the few employees of the new store, which by now also contained a warehouse, could no longer cope with the rush of customers. In particular, the delivery of products from the warehouse became such a test of endurance that the not-anymore-young entrepreneur was once again in demand as an unusual, strategic problem solver.

I guess that he was inspired by the food supermarkets that were just emerging in the USA—in any case, the outlets were quickly converted to a new self-service concept. An idea that was completely unusual in the industry, but which customers nevertheless accepted willingly. And once again, the entrepreneur turned this into a feature of his business, rewarding his hardworking customers by now offering the resulting cost advantage for his high-quality products at even lower prices.

The final step that turned Ikea into an international furniture store, however, no longer came from the boss himself, but from employees: customers now always looked at the products live and helped themselves to many items in the warehouse. However, it turned out that some products were too large to be transported in the customers' cars. So when one of the employees came up with the idea of removing the legs of a table that wouldn't fit in the trunk even with a little coaxing, the last typical Ikea feature was born. From then on, the company consistently redesigned its products so that they were as space-saving as possible to transport—and yet easy to assemble.

Ingvar Kamprad has consistently met resistance with unusual measures—measures that he may have been inspired to take by observing trends in other industries—and has generated unique supply advantages for his company from the solutions.

Ikea: The Three Most Important Success Factors
These were the main factors behind Ikea's early success in its early years:

- Lateral thinking. From the very beginning, Ingvar Kamprad has always looked for unusual, precisely non-obvious solutions.
- Proper benchmarking. Most companies and industries tend to use their competitors as a comparison and for brainstorming—and thus always stay in the same environment. Here, too, Ingvar Kamprad has generated a lot of innovation by looking sideways at other industries.
- Elasticity. Kamprad did not try to make his customers conform to his business models; on the contrary, he continuously questioned his business model and adapted it to his customers.

For the sake of completeness, it should be mentioned here that this list only describes Ikea's early years. Today, the company is no longer a start-up or medium-sized enterprise, but a multinational corporation that is pursuing completely different strategies for the future.

3.7 Shell: There Is More than One Future

Imagine you are sitting in a small meeting room with no windows. For hours you have been discussing future sales of a brand new product group that has just been created with your counterpart at the Asian headquarters. This is extremely little fun—despite sushi lunch on plastic plates from the delivery service—when there are chasms between the wish and the reality.

In one of my last positions as a salaried manager, I was responsible for such a completely new product group and had to quickly submit halfway reliable planning figures with which our factories were to plan and produce quantities in line with the market. But how could that be done? No one in the market had any sales experience with this type of product. Nevertheless, our Asian headquarters insisted on reliable figures during the planning meeting. A pointless battle of different cultures, in the course of which my American colleague got carried away and wanted to ask his cleaning lady at home—after all, she could "invent" such figures just as well as he could.

As the person responsible for the European market, I had a somewhat easier time of it: I was able to get estimates from our 30 European national branches, eliminate the worst errors with a few mathematical tricks and a lot of Excel, and thus deliver target figures that were significantly better than those of the Americans. But "good" was still something else. What we planned—and what we then actually sold—came from two worlds.

The colleagues at Royal Dutch Shell must have had a similar experience—only without Excel—when they introduced a system in 1965 that they called Unified Planning Machinery (UPM). Here, too, the goal was to be able to better control cash flow at the end of the day through more reliable financial planning. Their result, too, was as devastating as my numbers: The UPM system was supposed to make it possible to plan six-year periods at Shell, but already after the first period they stopped operations at the beginning of the 1970s—because of unsuccessfulness! The deviations between plan and reality were too great, and Shell's management felt little desire to make commitments based on such figures.

So purely numerical forecasts worked as little then as they do now. Fortunately for Shell, however, there had been another initiative in the course of thinking about the UPM system, which also ran from 1965 onwards. An initiative that to this day sets Shell apart from all other major oil companies. If you look at the group's website (Shell 2017), you will find vast amounts of future studies that Shell has produced and published on a wide variety of topics. In addition to results on energy and transport development, which reflect the group's core competence, there are also references to exotic topics that the Shell scenario team has worked on, for example, on the threat of AIDS (2005 for the UN) or the development of South Africa after the end of apartheid (1992 for Global Business Network).

What is special about this example is the methodological procedure that Shell developed for this purpose back in the 1960s. No predictions of the future were developed, but rather a wide variety of scenarios for a question that had only one thing in common: it had to be possible to develop them logically from different starting assumptions. How probable such scenarios were initially of no concern to the creators of the studies because the aim was by no means to offer shell management a reasonably safe path into the future. The aim of the scenarios was rather to stimulate the imagination of Shell's management and to catapult it out of its usual channels. What was wanted was for the company to develop a willingness to see a variety of conceivable developments in the future as possible—to be able to react flexibly as a result.

"Our goal was not to predict the future," says Jeremy Bentham, the current head of the Shell research group, "but to enable leadership to make more informed decisions via a better understanding of key drivers and key uncertainties." (Shell 2012b, p. 30). Indeed, even at the group's inception, it had been recognised that a lack of imagination in decision-making was a major cause of poor decisions.

As in many companies, there was also a tendency at Shell for decision-makers to anticipate a kind of "business as usual" as a picture of the future—an exceedingly human peculiarity based on the so-called optimism bias: We tend to want to see familiar patterns and are blind to unexpected developments. So, business as usual!

"Deep in our hearts, we would all choose a scenario without any surprises," Pierre Wack, the inventor of the Shell scenario technique, is said to have once commented (Shell 2012a, b, p. 39). However: even the scenario technique is not a panacea. Scenarios need to be reviewed regularly, as the 2014 New Lens Scenarios study (Shell 2014) shows: According to this study, it is expected to take until the year 2070 for passenger cars with internal combustion engines to completely disappear from our roads. A scenario that seems very unlikely because of the changes brought about in particular by the VW diesel scandal: for example, the Swedish carmaker Volvo declared in July 2017 that from 2019 onwards it would only present new vehicles that would be equipped with battery or hybrid drive systems (Spiegel Online 2017). In Norway, the share of pure diesel or petrol-burning cars in new registrations was already below 50% in June 2017 (Sorge 2017)—and the trend continues to fall. And finally, in mid-July 2017, the governments of France and the UK (FAZ 2017) declared their intention to ban the sale of diesel or petrol-powered vehicles altogether from 2040. Not even hybrids will have a chance then. But, as it is already formulated in a Shell video: "Scenarios are stories about the future, but they are not predictions"! (Shell 2012a, b)

Shell: The Three Most Important Success Factors

- Shell realised extremely early on that the future cannot be calculated mathematically.
- In addition, there was the realisation that decision-makers in companies need the inspiration to be able to assess the future in all its diversity.
- From all of this, the pioneering method of the scenario technique was developed.

3.8 Rügenwalder Mühle: Innovation Can Be Planned

It's hard to believe that the following sentences are supposed to come from someone whose family has been making a living from finished meat products for 180 years.

> Nutritionally, the sausage is not such a hoot. Apart from the fact that sausage is undoubtedly a tasty thing, there is not much positive to praise about it.
>
> CEO Christian Rauffus in an interview with the FAZ (Grossarth 2016)

The *Rügenwalder Mühle* is a medium-sized company, as there are hundreds of them in Germany—and yet again not. Originally founded as a family business in Poland (a village called Rügenwalde, today: Darłowo), the butchery company became one of the best-known suppliers of finished meat products such as sliced meats and spreads, sausages and meatballs. Like all meat-processing food companies, the company had been facing increased criticism of the production of the "raw material meat" for many years. More and more people wanted to limit or even completely give up their meat consumption in favour of a good conscience. A trend that could have ended disastrously for a small company (compared to the size of competitors such as Nestlé or Wiesenhof) like Rügenwalder Mühle, since despite great brand recognition, they hardly had enough resources to counter such a trend on their own.

Now, they could have tried to solve that problem by adapting to the usual market trends and simply putting even more "naturally produced" meat into their sausage. But that was not what owner Christian Rauffus and his managing director Godo Röben saw as a long-term solution for themselves personally and for the company. Godo Röben says in a personal interview (Röben 2017) about this: "Anyone who has ever seen a slaughterhouse from the inside just had to start thinking." And so Rügenwalder Mühle began the project of competing with itself by getting the in-house product developers excited about developing concepts that were as close as possible to the previous meat products in appearance, feel, and taste—but could be produced purely vegetarian.

A process that demanded one thing above all from the management: almost infinite patience with the employees. The internal resistance at Rügenwalder was great—after all, the company was originally a butcher's shop. The idea that one would somehow have to work "against the sausage" was initially at odds with many colleagues. But the management had the strength and stamina to take the team along on the new journey in many discussions and presentations. The result of the development project was a variety of cold cuts, meatballs and sausages, some of which were so close to the original that even the biggest in-house skeptics could no longer tell them apart from the company's meat-based products in blind tests. And consumers also rewarded the efforts of the medium-sized company from Lower Saxony. Within 30 months of starting the project, the company was able to increase sales of these new products to 20% of its total sales: Rügenwalder Mühle is currently the market leader in vegetarian meat substitutes by a wide margin—even far ahead of corporations like Nestlé.

But the company headquarters in Bad Zwischenahn are not satisfied with that. In addition to other products that the test kitchen wants to create from milk, soy and protein, they are also following the development of synthetic meat very closely. "We are only at the beginning after all," Godo Röben tells me in an interview about the company's long-term goals. "We've only been researching for two and a half years. There will be many more products that we can make entirely without animal meat. But our know-how on how a good sausage should taste definitely belongs in there."

Owner Rauffus and managing director Röben were convinced from the start that they were on the right track and put all their eggs in one basket: The entire marketing budget was put into the new products and thus on "meat-free". "If we hadn't competed with ourselves now, someone else would have done it at some point," Röben concludes.

Rügenwalder: The Three Most Important Success Factors

- The management of Rügenwalder Mühle was itself the driver for innovative future planning.
- In addition, there was a willingness to question one's own previous business.
- From the very beginning, employees were involved in the future process in the best possible way.

3.9 Casio: Identifying and Exploiting Market Changes

Rügenwalder designed its vision of the future and was also a trendsetter due to its pioneering role in the market. Other developments, however, cannot be planned so well in advance. That our children (or were we?) would feed electronic animals and put them to bed, for example (Tamagotchi—remember?). Or that we would communicate on the highest diplomatic level with only 140 characters (Twitter). These were trends that only developed from the behavior of consumers themselves and definitely could not be planned in the long term.

It was much the same for the Japanese company Casio in 1993. Casio Computer Co. was founded in 1957 by four technology-minded brothers to build what would eventually become known as a pocket calculator. Since no terms were existing for today's calculators or PCs in any language back then, they named their project and the company a *computer* after the English term for counting. And so this company was probably one of the first in history to ever carry the product label "computer" in its name, even though it did not even make "real" computers until the mid-1980s. Many of the subsequent products were the results of developments in pocket calculators. The experience of building low-power LCDs, custom-programmed processors, and clocks for these calculators led to the creation of digital watches, for example. In 1988, Kazuo Kashio, the second oldest of the four brothers, took over the management of the company. KK, as he was known in-house, was a passionate product developer who, over the years, had a large number of new product lines with sometimes adventurous features developed and marketed.

As digital technology became cheaper and cheaper—and digital watches were available for ridiculous prices—KK focused on diversification. Casio watches were filled with microcomputers and sensors and, decades before the invention of smart watches, were able to manage addresses and appointments, display air pressure and current altitude, measure blood pressure, or time events to 1/1000 of a second. In this way, Casio raised the average selling price of its digital watches well above the average of its cheap competitors, but even the Casio digital watches of the 1980s were not necessarily elegant watches, measured by the consumer tastes of the time. And so the Casio brand name became undeservedly synonymous with "cheap" digital watches. Although the company had a nine percent market share in the German watch market at the end of the 1980s according to GfK, it was still only the second-largest brand in the watch trade. The Swiss company Swatch, with its technically very simple but colourful analogue watches, took the cake with a market share of over 20%. This situation did not seem to change over the years, despite steadily increasing advertising expenditure and quite creative marketing measures that were quite unusual for Japanese companies; Casio remained number 2 in the watch segment by a wide margin.

However, the Japanese company had another previously untapped treasure: Since the company earned its money mainly in the B2C sector at the time, it had established an extremely lean organization with open doors and very short decision-making paths. Information was able to spread more quickly throughout the group, and employees and managers alike were able to build up a broader understanding of the market situation. Through this constellation, something happened that very rarely succeeds: Casio realized long before its target group that something was emerging among consumers that could potentially be exploited through clever marketing. The signs were very tentative, but the company took notice:

- In Shibuya, the trendy district of Tokyo at the time, a certain extremely chunky and resistant Casio watch, the G-Shock model, was increasingly bought in 1993.
- In London, a trendy magazine featured—quite unusually—another black Casio digital watch.
- The German scene magazine Tempo reported about decorative fashion accessories of the just establishing techno scene—with mentioned: Black digital watches.

It was only a few signs, scattered all over the globe, that made the marketers, and ultimately the company's management, scrap their marketing and production plans. Kazuo Kashio was known for his passion for creating new impulses anyway. And in Europe, too, the Japanese management mustered up the courage to follow the recommendations of the marketing crews and went down completely new communication paths. With limited budgets but very precise, coordinated schedules, measures were planned that would today be described as first-class guerrilla marketing. For example, a product launch was organized in a cult dance club on Hamburg's Reeperbahn with a very "special" fashion show of the emerging techno scene. A famous historical singer (Hildegart Knef) sang from the tape, supported by a then still very unusual techno mix, an anchorman of the most famous German tv news show moderated live and otherwise rather conservative watch dealers, journalists and the weirdest part of the weird Hamburg scene celebrated together through the night. Today, something like this might sound almost normal. Back then—and especially for a Japanese company—it was by no means.

The measures were first-class because they were successful: With these actions, Casio had turned the technology of extremely shock-resistant and waterproof digital watches, which had been languishing economically for over 10 years, into a trend: The G-Shock watches, previously sold only a few thousand times a year, became the brand's bestseller and changed the company's image immensely. So much so that the "cheap" digital watches of the 80s are now trendy design elements of Japanese youth as replicas in the Tokyo districts of Shibuya and Shinjuku.

But the prudent look into the future also paid off financially: with the G-Shock, Casio became the market leader in terms of value in the wristwatch sector and increased its average sales prices considerably: while before the G-Shock wave even expensive Casio watches were available for the equivalent of 100 EUR, today the top models are priced at almost 3000 EUR. And the fact that the company was then able to move its headquarters from a rented office in an skyscraper in Tokyo to its own building a few years later was certainly no coincidence either: Clever handling of the future pays off—even in Japanese yen!

Casio: The Three Most Important Success Factors

- Extremely short paths for decisions and information have led to rapid action.
- Very vigilant market monitoring made it possible to identify market shifts at a very early stage.
- The company dared something new—even if the planned measures went beyond the culture of the company.

3.10 Apple: Acting Instead of Waiting

Can there be a guidebook on how to shape your entrepreneurial future without mentioning Apple and its founder Steve Jobs? Probably not. Judging by what happened to him in the first 20 years of his career, Steve Jobs probably would have had every reason to fear the future: Starting very successfully with a good idea, he made a momentous series of unfavorable decisions at Apple that left the company's future bleak, was declared "disposable," and then started a new business with NeXT Computer, which never really took off business-wise. After so many stumbles along the way, people and organizations in corporations usually tend to be more cautious—exceedingly understandably so. If there isn't already a pronounced fear of the future, then you often find at least a wait-and-see attitude. Not so with Steve Jobs.

Now I am not an uncritical Apple disciple. I am critical of many of Steve Jobs' actions. But you can only take your hat off to the way Jobs dealt with the future. Even after the NeXT bankruptcy, he—back at Apple—was again fully committed to radical innovation. Along the way, he had a number of fundamental principles:

- So he was firmly convinced that it would not be worthwhile to run after the future. That's why Jobs invested very little in researching possible developments in the future.
- He also saw little point in spending money on market research. Instead, Jobs focused on shaping the future according to his own ideas. He gave the PC divi-

sion new impetus with the colorful iMac and began the attack on the music industry with the iPod and iTunes, which in turn would never have expected a competitor outside of its closest competitors.
- However, Jobs'most ingenious move in actively dealing with the future was probably the creation of the iPhone. And by that I don't just mean that this product created a new category that changed the world. Moreover, it proved the concept, that it pays off when one tries to compete himself early enough.

When he returned to Apple in 1997, Jobs had found a virtually meaningless company that had made a loss of almost US$1.5 billion the previous year and was on the verge of bankruptcy. In the decade that followed, up until the unveiling of the iPhone in 2007, Apple had long since returned to being a hugely successful brand, turning seven billion US dollars in sales into one billion in profits. More than half of that revenue—50.5% (MacPrime 2017)—came from Apple's earbud hard drive, as critics initially disparagingly referred to the iPod.

Now please try to put yourself in Steve Jobs'shoes, in the time about 1 year before the presentation of the iPhone. Presumably, hot and intense meetings were held at Apple to discuss what features to include in the eventual iPhone: The first speculations that Apple would be working on a mobile phone had leaked out, and more than a few financial analysts, market experts and other prophets doubted that this product would have a real chance in the market, given Nokia's incredible dominance. And then this already risky product should also have all the features of the iPod, then Apples core product? That would negatively impact the sales of the product and thus the company as a whole. Moreover, this move opened a door for all mobile phone vendors to attack Apple's core business!

In retrospect, the critics were right about one thing: iPod sales degenerated into a niche product with the iPhone. From over 50% of the company's revenue in 2006, it fell to a traumatic 0.97% at the end of 2014—the last year Apple even disclosed that product's revenue. Since 2015, the iPod has not been reported as a product at all in the company's published statistics.

Let's be honest: Would you have made this decision? To deliberately attack a product that accounts for over half of your total sales with a new idea—without knowing whether this new idea would even have a chance with your customers? What a difference to Kodak, which lets a future technology disappear in the basement to prevent competition to its products!

So Steve Jobs seems to have had a clear strategy for the future. But wasn't that just luck? Do you remember the example of the poker-playing monkey Sect. 2.3? The one whose superior abilities as a poker player could only have been confirmed with scientific precision by further experimentation? In the case of Apple, one can conclude from the accumulation of successful product launches that the Jobs strategy was planned at the time and did indeed work out. And as if to confirm this, Apple has currently lost its innovative power: while the company created four ground-breaking product categories during Jobs'active period between 2001 and 2010, practically only updates of these products have been introduced since the founder's death—except the iWatch, which has not yet achieved a significant share of Apple sales.

Apple: The Three Most Important Success Factors

- Apple, in the period described, was always itself the biggest competitor and continuously questioned its business models.
- Steve Jobs had clear visions of what he wanted to offer customers.
- Apple was mercilessly consistent in its actions. Strategies were not abandoned even if they did not immediately lead to great success.

3.11 Learning from the Past? Yes. Prediction? No!

Stories—or as we like to call them in marketing "case studies"—have a great charm, because, told in sufficient detail, the insights seem so obvious. And I'm sure that there will be plenty of similar examples in your industry as well.

But be careful: If you want to conclude your actions from such stories of your own, I advise you to analyse the facts extremely carefully and to interpret them just as carefully. Research carefully and in many directions before you work with them. It is too great a temptation to fall for the errors of hindsight discussed in the previous chapters based on a few seemingly obvious facts.

No matter what your method for preparing for the future: The most important issue is that your company's leadership and organization are so convinced of the path you've taken that it can no longer be lightly questioned or changed. For hardly any mistake destroys entrepreneurial success more frequently than that of fickleness. If you expect immediate and overwhelming success from a strategy for the future, you run the risk of stamping out a new orientation, a new product group, or a new communication strategy before it can even take effect.

Escape the supermarket checkout dilemma: No matter which checkout you choose, others lure you with all their might. But it is a statistical truth that you just don't win by changing the checkout. The same would happen to you if you continuously change your strategy. If you were convinced that you had chosen a good path, you should stay true to it. In all likelihood, you will be no less successful than if you had chosen another good path and followed it.

References

Buttlar H von (2015) Casio gibt Kameramarkt in Europa auf. http://www.capital.de/dasmagazin/casio-gibt-kamerageschaeft-in-europa-auf-4487.html. Zugegriffen: 20. Mai 2020

Eglau HO (1991) Countdown in Wilhelmshaven: Auch Daimler-Benz konnte den traditionsreichen Büromaschinenhersteller nicht retten. http://www.zeit.de/1991/41/countdown-in-wilhelmshaven/komplettansicht. Zugegriffen: 20. Mai 2020

Estrin J (2015) Kodak's first digital moment. https://lens.blogs.nytimes.com/2015/08/12/kodaks-first-digital-moment/. Zugegriffen: 20. Mai 2020

FAZ (2017) Auch Großbritannien will Diesel und Benziner komplett verbieten. http://www.faz.net/aktuell/wirtschaft/diesel-affaere/grossbritannien-verbietet-ab-2040-diesel-und-benzin-autos-15122531.html. Zugegriffen: 20. Mai 2020

Grossarth J (2016) Ein Wurstfabrikant will weg vom Fleisch. http://www.faz.net/aktuell/wirtschaft/unternehmen/ruegenwalder-muehle-will-trend-zur-vegetarischen-wurst-ausbauen-14527466.html. Zugegriffen: 20. Mai 2020

Kuhn T (2015) Ausstieg aus Kamera-Geschäft. http://www.wiwo.de/technologie/samsung-ausstieg-aus-kamera-geschaeft/12619746.html. Zugegriffen: 20. Mai 2020

MacPrime (2017) Apple Geschäftszahlen: analysen und Grafiken zum Umsatz, Gewinn und Verkaufszahlen seit 2000. https://www.macprime.ch/wissen/article/apple-geschaeftszahlen-analysen-grafiken-umsatz-gewinn-verkaufszahlen. Zugegriffen: 20. Mai 2020

Maschke T (2012) Olympus: "Zurück zu den Wurzeln". http://www.photoscala.de/2012/06/08/olympus-zurueck-zu-den-wurzeln/. Zugegriffen: 20. Mai 2020

Photoscala (2012) Samsung stellt Fabrik auf spiegellose Systemkameras um. http://www.photoscala.de/2012/05/14/samsung-stellt-fabrik-auf-spiegellose-systemkameras-um/. Zugegriffen: 20. Mai 2020

Photoscala (2016a) Fujifilm Geschäftszahlen: Mit analoger Fotografie zum Erfolg. http://www.photoscala.de/2016/07/29/fujifilm-geschaeftszahlen-mit-analoger-fotografie-zum-erfolg/. Zugegriffen: 20. Mai 2020

Photoscala (2016b) Halbjahresbericht vorgelegt: Nikon in der Krise. http://www.photoscala.de/2016/11/08/halbjahresbericht-vorgelegt-nikon-in-der-krise/. Zugegriffen: 20. Mai 2020

Photoscala (2017a) Abgesagt: Nikon DL-Serie kommt nicht auf den Markt. http://www.photoscala.de/2017/02/13/abgesagt-nikon-dl-serie-kommt-nicht-auf-den-markt/. Zugegriffen: 20. Mai 2020

Photoscala (2017b) Nikon will sich auf profitable Systemkameras konzentrieren. http://www.photoscala.de/2017/02/27/nikon-will-sich-auf-profitable-systemkameras-konzentrieren/. Zugegriffen: 20. Mai 2020

Photoscala (2017c) Ricoh richtet Kamerasparte neu aus. http://www.photoscala.de/2017/04/13/ricoh-richtet-kamerasparte-neu-aus/. Zugegriffen: 20. Mai 2020

Röben B (2017) Interview mit Bodo Göben am 31. Mai 2017 in Bad Zwichenahn
Shell (2012a) Windows on the future: modeling scenarios. https://www.youtube.com/watch?v=l4MDcGYif4k. Zugegriffen: 27. Jun 2020
Shell (2012b) 40 Years of shell scenarios. https://www.shell.com/promos/forty-years-of-shell-scenarios/_jcr_content.stream/1448557479375/a0e75f042fee5322b72780ee36e5ba17c35a4fc6/shell-scenarios-40yearsbook080213.pdf. Zugegriffen: 20. Mai 2020
Shell (2014) New lenses on the future, Seite 34. https://www.shell.com/energy-and-innovation/the-energy-future/scenarios/new-lenses-on-the-future/_jcr_content/par/relatedtopics.stream/1519787281108/a368f1a2e9a16326855951c3879b323408ee323a/nls-web-german-brochure.pdf?. Zugegriffen: 20. Mai 2020
Shell (2017) Shell Scenarios. http://www.shell.com/energy-and-innovation/the-energy-future/scenarios.html. Zugegriffen: 20. Mai 2020
Sorge NV (2017) Anteil von Elektro- und Hybridautos in Norwegen steigt auf 53 Prozent. http://www.manager-magazin.de/unternehmen/autoindustrie/norwegen-elektroauto-anteil-steigt-auf-53-prozent-a-1157126.html. Zugegriffen: 20. Mai 2020
Spiegel Online (2017) Volvo verabschiedet sich vom Verbrennungsmotor. http://www.spiegel.de/auto/aktuell/volvo-verabschiedet-sich-ab-2019-vom-verbrennungsmotor-a-1156009.html. Zugegriffen: 20. Mai 2020
WeltN24 (2012) Kodaks geheimer Atomreaktor in Gebäude 82. https://www.welt.de/wirtschaft/article106324750/Kodaks-geheimer-Atomreaktor-in-Gebaeude-82.html. Zugegriffen: 20. Mai 2020
Wikipedia (2017) Tim Berners-Lee. https://de.wikipedia.org/wiki/Tim_Berners-Lee. Zugegriffen: 20. Mai 2020

Dealing with Changing Markets

4

Abstract

When it comes to future strategies, it is not enough to develop a good prediction of the expected changes. Rather, market changes, but also changes within companies, follow very specific rules that need to be taken into account during the future process. The most important logics of such changes are outlined in this chapter.

Imagine for a moment that you want to walk to the next village (= destination) and that you have already sketched a route on the map (= strategy). Which method do you use to get to your destination? Whether you arrive safe and sound depends not only on the quality of your strategy but also on the condition of the path. If the road is well paved, you will make good progress by car, motorbike or bicycle. If it's a boggy road, you might be better off wearing wellies and walking. And if your route takes you to a river or large lake, swimming costumes might be in order.

To select the right strategy and—derived from this—also the implementation tactics, it is therefore important to deal with the framework conditions that you will encounter on your way. So let's take a look at the most important rules of the game of changing markets.

H. Hilbig, *Shaping the Future of Your Business*,
https://doi.org/10.1007/978-3-658-35349-0_4

4.1 Three Types of Changes: Evolution, Revolution, Disruption

When training for my driver license, my driving instructor always warned me that rail crossing with barrierswere the really dangerous ones because everyone expected danger at the unrestricted rail crossings and was accordingly careful. At rail crossing with barriers, however, most people rely on the barriers as a warning signal—which can quickly become a fatal mistake if they don't work as planned. This warning worked. At open gated level crossings, I take extra care to check the track before I drive—almost more so than at ungated crossings. The same principle applies to the seemingly simple, safe market changes: At almost every convention or congress there is a speaker who warns the audience about *disruptive technologies,* technologies that can strip an existing and functioning market of the foundation of its rationale virtually overnight. Such speakers always get a lot of attention, as they are something like the doomsday prophets of the modern age: it only has to sound dramatic enough and be delivered with seemingly innovative vocabulary while wearing a black turtleneck pullover.

But those who always stare at the much-vaunted, dramatic dangers of digitalization, for example, overlook the fact that there are also other forms of change that may have even more radical effects while coming along much less spectacular.

Example

Just imagine for a moment a beautiful day at the North German Plain. On the coasts of the North Sea, land emerges from the water with beautiful, six-hour regularity, which tourists like to look at and open up with so-called mudflat hikes. The danger here is that on foot you can sometimes find yourself several kilometres from land—much further than you would swim back. If the water returns while you are still outside watching the funny lugworms build their castles, it can quickly threaten your existence.

Personally, I don't know anyone who would go out onto the mudflats if there is stormy weather announced. After all, that would be far too dangerous, wouldn't it? However, if there would be "only" a strong wind (which can also push the water back into the German Bight faster than usual), there are some brave people who go out for a bit. And there are even more who go Wadden hiking when a nice mild sunny day tempts them to do so.

And now guess which weather is the most dangerous? When does the sea rescue service have the most operations because of trapped waders? A little hint: You can find a hint for the solution in the railway gate example. ◄

So when we talk about changes that can influence markets, we must by no means talk only about disruptive changes—i.e., the hurricane—we must pay just as much attention to revolutionary changes (the west wind) and above all (!) to evolutionary movements (the normal tide when the sun is shining) if the water is not to take us by surprise. I therefore especially warn against the last, seemingly simple situation. Unlike disruptive and revolutionary changes in the market, evolutionary market changes take a very long time—so you could do well to adapt to them. Unfortunately, such changes also come so inconspicuously that many industries and companies don't even notice these changes for a long time—just like the tide quietly entering the tidal flats. And suddenly you're surrounded by water that, until now, has only gurgled gently and so sweetly.

A good example is the destruction of the classic camera market by smartphones—an example that was often used in industry presentations to explain the concept of *disruptive technologies*. Disruptive—this refers to a technology that greatly reduces or even completely displaces an existing solution due to better performance. PCs, which have replaced the typewriter, are such a *disruptive technology,* as are cars, which have largely—everywhere except in the centre of Vienna!—or the CD, which has done away with the romantic crackle of the record.

But let's take a closer look at the case of cameras: In terms of technology, cameras inside of smartphones were not a new technology at all: sensor, lens and image processing were largely identical to a normal compact camera—only of significantly poorer quality[1] until a few years ago. This part of the technology therefore does not meet the requirements of *disruptive* technologies.

So, just the functions that a smartphone has, but a camera does not, remain: sending pictures by e-mail or being able to upload them to social network platforms. However, since the decline in the camera market not only affected compact products, i.e., small snapshot cameras, but also high-end system and SLR cameras sold much worse than before, the question arises whether an enthusiastic photo fan who was previously prepared to invest several thousand euros for a system camera would let such features influence his buying and usage behaviour? Would a convinced SLR user stop buying new high-end cameras just because his smartphone can also send significantly worse pictures? You need a lot of rhetorical skills to derive a credible story for this.

Lastly, there is the time factor: disruptive changes should also have a stormy character—and the ones we know currently becoming even faster:

[1] In 2014, for example, the average resolution of camera modules in smartphones worldwide was 6.6 megapixels. In the same period, digital cameras had an average of 16.2 megapixels (see. GfK 2014).

- The car has replaced horse-drawn carriages (and therefore horse manure!) within 20 years.
- The fax took another 10 years to replace the telex.
- The PC replaced the typewriter within 5 years.
- And it took the smartphone a whole 2 years to replace the conventional mobile phone. Just ask Nokia—they've weathered this storm!

And now let's look back to cameras and smartphones again: Individual cell phones with camera functions have been around since 1998, while smartphones have always had these modules built-in since the first iPhone in 2007. A radical, disruptive impact on the classic camera market would therefore be expected from 2008 or 2009 at the latest. But nothing happened: for five more years, smartphones and their camera function had no impact on camera sales at all—on the contrary: camera numbers also grew, reaching new records year after year. And system cameras even climbed from record to record for 7 years after Steve Jobs' legendary keynote.

Seven years that technology in a different form has no negative impact on a similar, existing one—can you still call that a disruptive technology? Is that *disruptive*? Even for a normal, revolutionary change—a west wind -, 7 years would be far too long. So, the shift from cameras to smartphones has been rather leisurely, which argues for an evolutionary shift. And for the danger of such evolutionary changes. Because after five decades of continuous growth, the providers of classic photography have felt secured—as acting in and controlling a stable market.

Most typical market models, such as Michael Porter's "Four Corner Concept" (Porter 2013), assume that in stable markets there is a relatively stable equilibrium of market participants—a view that most managers in such markets would probably also quickly affirm. But such equilibria are deceptive because markets are often stable only in the absence of alternative options: Even if at least one of the market participants is dissatisfied in some way, usually he has no choice to change. However, as soon as the entry of a new competitor, a new business model or a new technology offers an alternative option, the market changes.

In many technical product categories, we see exactly this effect. There, it is the consumers who have no choice: Who among us hasn't grumbled about the complex usability of VCRs, Windows Vista, or said cameras? But as soon as a serious purchasing alternative emerges, this hidden imbalance becomes obvious—and customers change horses.

- *Before:* Anyone who wanted to take pictures (and who didn't?) had no choice: One had to get a camera—even if that included a lot more complexity than most buyers wanted to use.
- *After:* If you own a smartphone, the resulting images come close to quality to your demands, the phone is easy to use, and you don't feel that you invested for functions that you do not use anyway.

Creeping: Evolutionary changes are so dangerous because market participants do not notice them for a long time. And when the change does occur, the "completely surprised" protagonists are unclear about the cause. Could it be that this is why the few new cameras still see the light of day still with ten or more switches, buttons and dials, while the (technically much more powerful) smartphones manage with just one?

4.2 People, Technology and Business Models

If you take a closer look at the success stories of Apple founder Steve Jobs, you will come to the surprising realization that everything that he has led to great success as products already existed before—we already talked about this in Sect. 3.10. But why exactly did an equally great innovator like Bill Gates fail to make his much earlier tablet a success, while Steve Jobs seemed to have it easy? Why were Nokia or Blackberry not successful with high-end mobile phones, while Jobs'first iPhone went through the roof?

In both cases, the functionality of the devices was similar—Apple's offering may have been slightly more technically advanced—but that didn't explain the extraordinarily different successes. A realization that is a real cold shower for all developers who believe in the pure power of technology. And a clear rejection of the feature-loving brochures of the electronics markets: More function does not automatically sell better!

So what made the iPhone, iPod and iPad so much more successful? The answer seems as simple as it is obvious: it was the usability of the products—the GUI (graphical user interface), technologically speaking. With the iPhone, people held a computer filled to the brim with technology in their hands for the first time, requiring nothing more than simple swipes and taps. The whole thing was so intuitively designed that you only had to delve deeper into the functionality when you were ready. But the beginning was so simple that even three-year-olds could operate these products—and still can today.

Wondering if that's all there is to it? Do you still have a working camera lying around at home? How deep did you ever get into the operation of that camera? Did you ever fully understand the differences in the little dial with the letters S, A and P? And if that camera was expensive when you bought it—more than 250 US$, to give you a figure—didn't you somehow always feel guilty because you never took the time to get deeper into it? How much better could your photos from the last long-distance holiday have been, if only you had ... And now the question: Have you ever had a similarly guilty conscience because you never bothered to look deeper into the photo app of your 700 US$ smartphone?

You are closer to your smartphone because it offers you solutions where other products give you problems in handling. It offers you an emotional(!) advantage over other technically comparable solutions. In 2006 the three sociologists Barnekow, Sven and Braun-Thürmann, Holger wrote about this: (Barnekow et al. 2006)

> Sociology would be responsible for the interface management between producers and potential users in the development process and for analysing existing innovation projects for cultural gaps. [...] In this context, these findings can be used not only ex-post for possible reconfiguration after the market launch, as in the case study, but above all prospectively in an initial phase of innovation genesis to link more application-oriented design options back to the developers.

In other words, people have always struggled with technology that was difficult to understand or use. In addition to the technology itself, the acceptance of the product by the people who are supposed to use it plays the second major role for an offer that is supposed to change a market as a game-changer one day. By the way, I'm not sure if Steve Jobs would ever have invented his wiping technique if a sociologist had advised him and pointed out "cultural gaps".

But there is a third factor that plays a role in the question of whether a new offering will revolutionize a market or not: filthy lucre! An idea may be as advanced as it is and be readily accepted by people—if there is no viable business model for it, the provider of this solution will dry up financially. Just think for a moment about the alarming situation that hardly anyone is willing to pay for information on the Internet—newspaper publishers are therefore still looking for a good, working business model! This was also the case for the small start-up Google Inc. in 1998: They had a brilliant idea how to build a search engine for the Internet that would eclipse everything that had been done before and make content suddenly findable all over the world, but how could they earn money with it? A dollar per search term, please? It took two more years before the problem was solved and the first 350 advertisers were able to use the beta version of an ad selling service—Google AdWords (Wikipedia 2020).

So if you are looking for the future of your market and want to develop the right strategy for your company, you should first take a critical look at these three questions:

- Is your planned offer really (technically) feasible?
- What does your planned offering provide to gain broad emotional acceptance from your target audience?
- Do you have a resilient business model?

4.3 Future you Have Overlooked?

Of course, it makes perfect sense to think about the future direction of your industry and your business—a journey that can be a long, rocky road, depending on your industry. However, before you embark on this journey (definitely do!), be sure to check out two shortcuts that can bring you new business, even in the short term.

On the one hand, there are unused opportunities in the current business: While I am writing this book, department store chains are complaining publicly that they do not have the same opportunities as online shops and are therefore demanding more frequent Sunday opening. This is a paradoxical situation since only a few years ago hardly any of these shop operators believed in the future of online business. The MediaMarkt chain, for example, only took serious steps towards setting up an online shop under pressure from the market—and possibly therefore much too late. Internal coordination problems delayed the launch almost indefinitely. By then, however, the chain was already losing market share year after year. And like MediaMarkt, it was the same for many retailers. At best, they operated online shops half-heartedly alongside their retail stores. To date, only a few operators have combined the advantages of the physical offer in the store with those of the online shop and established strategic omnichannel. And I don't just mean the rather harmless buy-online-and-pick-up-at-store principle: real omnichannel solutions look much smarter than the multichannel solutions currently implemented by many parallel operators.

So today's Sunday-opening demanders haven't thought about the future for years, don't take advantage of the benefits that physical stores offer compared to pure online platforms, and instead demand legislative changes to preserve their business model …

Before you set out to shape your future, you should be sure that your company has correctly identified the opportunities that already exist today and is taking advantage of them. Without taking this step, you run the risk that opportunities that arise in the future process will also be overlooked—or worse, dismissed as science fiction—by the colleagues or management involved.

The second "shortcut" to new business then again has more directly to do with the future. Is there a new business model or a new trend in your industry? Look not only in the direction of the domestic German market but also in the direction of Japan, the USA and Great Britain. Many changes arise in one of these three markets and then spill over into other countries with a time lag, so to speak. You can use this time to be the first to export such ideas to other markets. The time you have to do this depends on the product and the degree of spread of a trend. A consumer trend from the UK or the USA can take a year before it arrives in Central Europe—from Asia, it can take longer. And 2 years can pass before such developments reach Hungary, Italy, or Israel. This process takes even longer in the area of B2B products or services.

In this way, you are already helping to shape the future today—even if it may not be where you normally do business.

4.4 More Precise Planning through Feedback Loops

We have already talked about Philip Tetlock several times. He was the US scientist with infinite patience who could wait 20 years to find out whether any of his experts had predicted anything halfway senseful. This same Philip Tetlock also says the essential sentence about forecasting in his book *Super Forecasting* (Tetlock and Gardner 2016, p. 23):

> In most cases, predictions are made and then nothing happens. It's rarely checked to see how correct they were, and certainly not with sufficient regularity and scientificity to draw any conclusions.

Even though you may not start planning for the future until you have finished reading this book, your company is already planning and forecasting now. Don't you use Excel and PowerPoint to look forward to the coming year (or even longer periods)? This is probably a common practice in all companies.

So, do you think these spreadsheet marvels are even halfway true to the reality of the following year in your business? If you've never checked, I recommend you do this exercise for fun: Take last year's precisely pre-planned values and superimpose them over the result a year later. It probably won't surprise you if I predict that your numbers will all be no better than Tetlock's monkey at darts. And no, no matter what you do, you will never (!) be able to deliver (or be delivered, if you are in the unenviable position of having to commission such planning figures) perfect forecasts. We should have gotten that far in this book: there can be no such thing as a perfect forecast—not even with Excel. But ...

Example

Why not look forward to your next holiday for a brief moment? The day of departure is approaching and you start packing your suitcase. The weather forecast predicts sunny weather with daytime highs of 16 °C. What are you packing? Or better yet, what don't you pack? The swimming trunks, for example. Or the short-sleeved shirts and shorts (dear reader: please translate this bulleted list to female clothing if needed—I'm just more familiar with male suitcases). You will rather take spring clothes and of course "something warm"—after all, it could be noticeably cooler in the morning and evening.

But what if I were to tell you now that the temperature figure in the weather forecast is by no means a certain value, but, just like the rain forecast, for example, only a figure with a certain probability? So it could be colder as well as warmer than 16 degrees. This has a great influence on your case, because it would be good to know in which order of magnitude the meteorologists are uncertain about the temperature and how far it can therefore deviate from the said 16°C. If we talk about one degree more or less, this does not change the packing of your suitcase. But what if the temperature reading was only accurate to about 6°C? That would mean your holiday experience could fluctuate between a daily maximum temperature of 10°C or 22°C. No question: You would have to pack the really big suitcase to be prepared for these big differences.

So it is far less important to know the predicted temperature than the possible deviation from it. But exactly the same applies to your target figures for the coming year. You will never hit the exact sales volume per product and country. But you should try to determine the accuracy of the forecasts and, if necessary, improve them for the coming years. ◀

Just imagine that you receive a quantity plan for 1 year from three country managers. At the end of the year, you notice that two of them deviated very significantly from the plan, but the third one submitted a very good plan on average for all of his customers. Now you can reduce the error rate immediately by two simple methods:

- Mathematically, you could determine the mean deviation of the planning and in the coming year simply include this in the planning of the two "deviating" col-

leagues. You determine the extent of the human error, so to speak. Do this a few years in a row and you will have an ever-improving estimate of realistic planning figures.
- The second alternative is to play these error variables back to the colleagues every year. The sales manager, who always estimates significantly too high, thus becomes more cautious—and the one who plans too low, a little more courageous.[2]

Incidentally, Philip Tetlock used these two methods—in somewhat simplified form—to improve the overall quality of future forecasts. He looked for people who were right more often than average and linked their predictions mathematically.

So if you want to set out in your company to meet the future better prepared, I recommend starting with the regular comparison of all planning assumptions with the later reality. Please remember: There is nothing shameful about being off the mark with your market and business forecasts. You just need to know how far off the mark you were.

4.5 Is there a "Right" Mind-Set?

Up to this point, it has primarily been about methodology—about what you should know before you fall into avoidable traps in future management. However, successful change always starts in your own company. How one approaches market changes, which ways of working and thinking are customary or frowned upon in the company, plays a very significant role in this. From my work, but also the analysis of many successful—and even more non-successful—companies, a way of working has developed over the years that I would like to share with you.

4.5.1 Resilience: Stay Ready for the Change!

Let's start with a trait you really can't do without: Willingness to change. If you've read this section, I'm asking you to be honest about the changing status of your business: Are you willing to be critical of your beliefs and throw them overboard when necessary? Are your leaders and your employees on board with any neces-

[2] However, it is important that your company no longer pays out bonuses to sales colleagues only according to absolute target achievement - which the low planner always prefers - but that planning accuracy becomes part of the bonus calculation system.

sary new thinking? If you have the slightest doubt that you have not yet reached this first point, you should not take further steps yet, because you will not achieve a good result for your future process. This is similar to the situation back then on the three-meter board in the public swimming pool: As long as you don't stand up there with the right attitude, jumping is no fun!

There are certainly markets that seem to be stable for a seemingly long time. Only when you look back you do realize that such markets have also changed drastically. If you are active in such a market, try to imagine briefly what was different 30 or 40 years ago: Which products, which technologies did not exist back then? How have customer structures, business models or even the "rules of the game", i.e., the rules of your market, changed?

I am just writing this book, so I don't have a chance to discuss this with you now, but I am sure that you can think of many examples of such changes. And this is already the most important insight on the way to good future management:

▶ Your market has changed constantly in the past. And that's why it will continue to change in the future.

This may sound banal, but it is in fact—as we have already seen at the beginning of the book—one of the biggest hurdles for many companies: The possoibility of a drastic change in one's own business is either fully refused or else expected so far in future that one does not need to deal with it now. However, this fundamental acceptance of the continuous change of your own market is the first important step that you have to take!

The second important success factor in the mindset of corporate management is something that various researchers agree on describing as resilience (Bhattarai 2018). In German literature, on the other hand, people like to talk about "flexibility", but this seems to me to fall short: resilience describes the ability and the desire of an organisation to stretch itself and in this way to adapt methods, tools and products far beyond the current situation when the market requires it.

A good example of elasticity in mindset is the mission statement attributed to Walt Disney for his company: He is said to have formulated as early as the 1960s that his company's mission was *to make people happy*. Only in this way was it possible to expand the range of (printed) comics to include films, TV, theme parks and musicals, thus opening up completely new markets. Just imagine if he had insisted that the company's core competence was drawing comics and, following the advice of many business consultants, he had fully focussed on that. Much of all that enchanting, commercially successful empire would never have come into being ...

The biggest hurdle to this goal of wanting to remain elastic as an organization—and personally as a leader—turns out to be one's experience. Because having experienced only means storing what you have experienced as a pattern and thus being able to retrieve it for future decisions. Someone with a lot of experience can therefore fall back on more patterns than someone who lacks this experience. Theoretically this helps, but—as we have already seen in the previous chapters—it increases the chance to fail: More experience means more patterns. And more patterns means more risk to limit the imagination when thinking about the future.

So be careful and beware of your knowledge and experience; it could be that they lead you to wrong assumptions. The examples of Kodak and Olympia, but also positively that of Rügenwalder, show how quickly you can win or fail on this first point alone. Or, to quote Albert Einstein:

► We can't solve problems by using the same kind of thinking we used when we created them.

4.5.2 The Never-Ending Story: Future Management Never Ends!

We have already talked about it: If you bought this book to devote yourself for once to the subject of the future and then have peace again for 10 years, I must disappoint you. Very bitterly, in fact. The future is constantly changing. Every new invention, every new service, every new offering creates new directions in business, and sometimes even events that have nothing to do with your business or industry have radical effects—Corona was the best example of an abrupt change in all global markets! So if you were hoping for a one-off process to make your business fit for the future, or even just to review your future strategy, please rethink now.

Until 2015, the general opinion in the automotive industry was that electromobility and autonomous driving still belonged in the realm of science fiction. The then CEO of Porsche Matthias Müller even spoke of hype on the subject of self-driving vehicles that was not justified by anything (Spiegel Online 2015). Only 2 years later, the diesel scandal at VW and others had such a drastic effect that, that there was suddenly increased discussion of electric vehicles and suspicious glances were cast at China, where the topic is now being tackled at full speed. And in 2019, e-mobility even became the VW Group's top priority.

And autonomous driving? On June 22, 2017, one of the first laws in the world came into force in Germany, allowing the use of self-driving vehicles under certain conditions. In 2018, the first self-driving buses were deployed in Hamburg. Oh, and Matthias Müller—who thought it was all hype—became CEO of VW supported for his company plans to provide self-driving car-sharing services under the brand name Sedric starting in 2021 (Grundhoff 2017). Within just 2 years, the assessment of the future of one of Germany's largest industries has changed completely!

So the future is changing faster than we are often aware of. If you want to prepare your company for this, you can only do so in a regular process that ensures that you recognize new developments—even insidious ones!—in good time and incorporate them into your strategy for the future. More important than operational preparation, however, is the mental attitude that a company brings to the new.

In the 1980s, Time/system was a kind of status symbol for almost all managers in central Europe—just like the *filofax* was in Anglo-Saxon countries. Those who climbed the hierarchy and became "important" were provided with a management planning calendar from their company. Basic price according to today's prices about 250 US$—in the executive leather variant from 600 US$—plus the necessary time management seminar from 1000 US$. There was practically no company of any standing left in which this self-planning tool was not available. By the early 1990s, it was at the height of its popularity and the decline began. With the first forerunners of the smartphone, digital organizers, and their linkage to the first, still quite rudimentary scheduling on PCs, the paper had largely become obsolete. The company still had an impeccable reputation—a valuable brand, one would say today—but could not bring itself to make a fundamental change in product policy. The opportunity to participate in the boom of electronic planning was missed because the management did not want to take the focus of business activities away from the DIN A5[3] sized original product: They did try many additional products—seminars, software, calendars with smaller formats—but they always saw them only as a supplement to the original system, never as an alternative for the future. Today, after various changes of ownership, the company is only a shadow of its former self.

▶ So when you set out on your future, establish a way of thinking and working that welcomes new things and lets employees and management alike be curious.

[3] The DIN A5 format calendar was the foundation of the company's success.

4.5.3 Involving Employees

So you have now decided to give more space to the idea of developing a future strategy for your company. Congratulations! However, the wrongest thing you can do now would be to consider which department you want to assign this task so that it would be quietly "done" somewhere in the basement of your office building. For one thing, as we will see later, the issue of managing the future is not the responsibility of any particular department. But for another, it is important that you quickly and expeditiously share the plan throughout the company (mind you, this is about making the intention known, not the results!).

In addition to motivating colleagues, this has an extremely important long-term effect: you abruptly increase your input for the planned process. As soon as the people in your company know that there exists a planned preparation for the future, they start to pass on any potentially interesting information to the project team. Instead of a few specialists having to scramble to find interesting developments, you suddenly have hundreds of eyes and ears gathering information from newspapers, TV, and the Internet. Think about the G-Shock example for a moment. It was only a few reports, scattered all over the world, whose input was put together into a vague picture at Casio. The trick, however, was not so much to recognize the pattern—we humans are really good at that—but to get this information in the first place.

▶ Also, pay attention to which of your employees contributes the most interesting information: he or she could become an important participant for your future management.

4.5.4 Thinking and Working Holistically

So your preparations for future management are in full swing, your employees know about it and are already providing your project team with all kinds of input on potentially interesting developments. But who do you give the project to now? Who should take care of it?

Marketing is always predestined for something like this. They are also creative enough to "spin around". On the other hand, you have to understand what technologies we have at our disposal. So it's more the product management … or better the finance department? They have a function called "strategic corporate planning" … The answer is preferably all of them—and a few more.

Of course, you have to have someone take responsibility for controlling a process like the one we will talk about later. But in any case, avoid the mistake of parking your company's future with a special department, as is common practice in corporations.

Example

I once worked in a company that had created a division called "NBD" (New Business Development) to bring development projects from our research departments to life and generate revenue. A real silo—as this area was not integrated into the business of the regular sales departments, there were few exchanges, and even fewer products migrated from the development stage into long-term sustainable business.

The result was that the sales departments only took on new ideas from NBD if they were promising and fitted into the usual prey scheme. After all, they weren't responsible for anything else—that's what NBD was for. NBD, in turn, did their utmost to generate maximum sales from every idea that became a product and, since the sales channels of the classic sales departments were of course taboo, they also entered any sales channel they could find—fully uncoordinated with sales department. A hopeless mess, which was frustrating for the employees of all departments and did not bring the company one step closer to a future perspective. The NBD division was dissolved at some point and none of the many, in part highly creative product concepts made it into the regular product range. ◀

The personnel limitations that most companies have compared to large international acting corporations are a positive effect on the planned process: Refrain from founding a future department and instead make your future project colorful. Mix as many experiences and views of your company as possible and integrate them into the processes. This is the only way to achieve a holistic view of your activities—and those of your competitors—as illustrated in the Casio example. And:

▶ For your project, look for the true lateral thinkers in your company—those who express unusual points of view even when it becomes uncomfortable.

The emphasis is on "true", because many companies nominally look for such employees in every second job advertisement, but then they tend to hire more conformist applicants whose lateral thinking skills are limited to spicing up Excel, Word and PowerPoint files with colourful charts and images. They won't help you with this task!

4.5.5 Developing Scenarios

We already know from Philip Tetlock that experts do little better than a chimpanzee at darts when it comes to the future. Because they make concrete (at least now and then!) predictions. Unfortunately, the future is becoming increasingly unclear in the distance and the number of possibilities of how the future could develop is growing—please remember this picture in Fig. 4.1!

So a forecast has only a small chance of actually coming true—and a very large chance of being wrong. That is one of the reasons why many self-proclaimed experts on the future like to remain vague, especially—as Philip Tetlock says—the more often they are seen on television and earn their money with it. Somehow the phrase about prophets who are not valid in their own country is strangely not at all true … Tetlock, therefore, recommends that if you still want to rely on experts, you should rely on those whose statements are concrete—and therefore verifiable.

"We will probably get along without cars in the future", for example, is a conceivably inaccurate prediction, because it does not even contain an indication of the time factor. All those who are now waiting for this prediction to come true could do so forever—without a target time, such a prediction can be correct (provided we

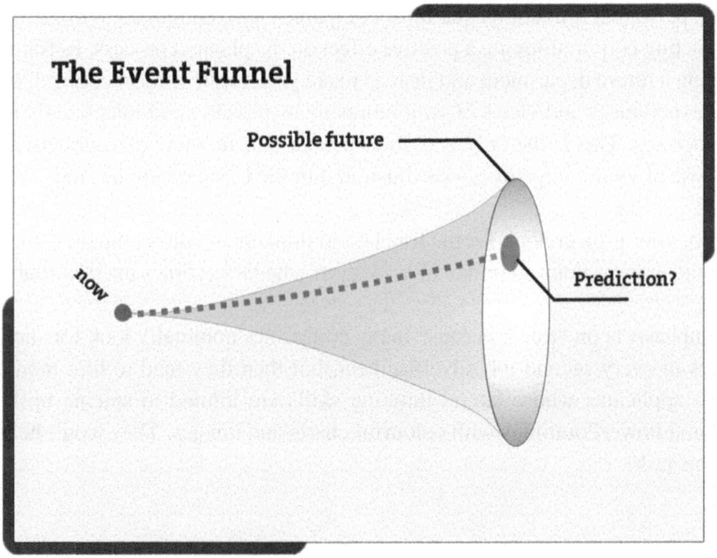

Fig. 4.1 Event funnel

should abolish cars tomorrow), but never wrong. Because as long as nothing happens, the prediction is still open—and that valid …

But other parts of the formulation are also not suitable to serve as a basis for future decisions: Cars—does this mean motor vehicle as we know them today, or also everything that will hover over the road in the future? If self-driving electric vehicles are called eMobs (or anything like this) in the future and the generation after next only knows the word *car* from old movies, was the forecast correct or not?

And then pay attention to the part that talks about probability. What do you mean by this statement, "A predicted event will likely occur"? Do you expect the prediction to occur 80% of the time? Or is 70% enough? If a situation has only two possibilities—either/or, so to speak—then even one possibility with a 51% hit rate is already more likely than the other. But is that enough for you as a "good" prediction?

A good prediction is therefore not one that could somehow and sometimes be interpreted as having come true, but one that delivers concrete and measurably formulated statements with a timeline. However, follwing the logic of the event funnel, such single-opointed predictions rarely come true. The oil company Royal Dutch Shell also recognised this in the 1960s and—as we have already discussed—replaced the simple forecast with a system that is now known as the scenario technique (see Fig. 4.2).

Instead of venturing a single prediction, the trick is to work out very precisely what external factors the development of your market or your industries might depend on, determine their conceivable changes ("rises", "falls"), and then look into the future in a strictly logical way through sensible combinations of such initial values. This sounds a bit theoretical, but in the end, it is not at all. Later you will see that this method can even be fun. The result is not a single prediction, but a series of predictions—scenarios—that can be used as the corner flags of a football field mentioned earlier: They show you roughly the playing field in which you should move—a process we call future framing.

▶ Beware of singular, one-off forecasts at all costs. Instead, develop meaningful and credible scenarios for your industry and your company, which you share with your employees and superiors in the form of understandable stories.

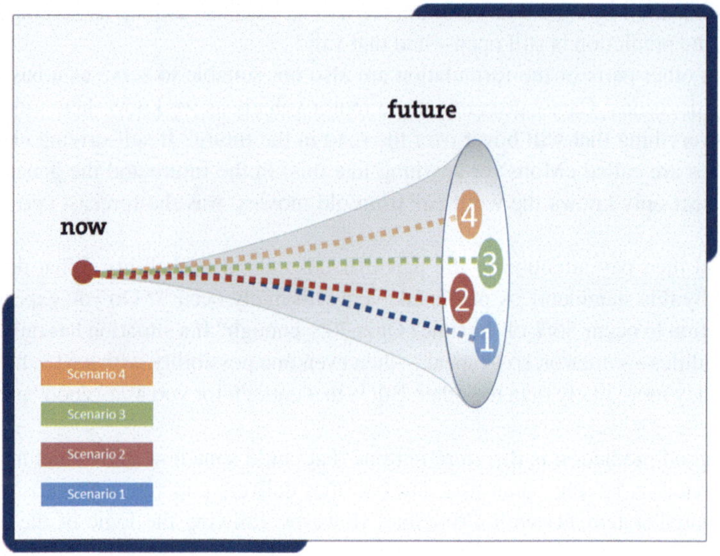

Fig. 4.2 The event funnel in the scenario technique

4.5.6 Your Customers Do Not Know the Future either

Steve Jobs did it. Henry Ford did it. Why don't you do the same? Ignore your customers when it comes to shaping the future of your company. Or, more accurately, ignore your customers' opinions about what the future might look like. Steve Jobs said in a Business Week interview in 1998 (Lange 2011), "It's very difficult to have marketing focus groups create products. Often people don't know what they want until you show it to them." And Henry Ford is quoted on the same topic as saying, "If I would have asked my customers beforehand what they wanted, they would have said 'faster horses".

Example

1996 was the year in which digital photography was to celebrate its breakthrough. On the occasion of the world's largest photo trade fair at the time, the Photokina in Cologne, Germany, a large number of companies presented digital cameras for the first time. The company I had just joined at the time also had a series of such products in the pipeline. And so, shortly before the trade fair, I flew around Europe with a suitcase full of "working samples", i.e., functioning prototypes, and accompanied so-called focus group interviews in the most important European markets. The results were devastating: none of the participating consumers had any real idea what he or she would do with a digital camera. The feature that got the most praise was the "ability to view pictures instantly" through the built-in LCD screen. But buy it? No, because of the expected prices of 1200 US$ upwards, the enthusiasm of the interviewees was rather limited, as the comparable compact film cameras of that time cost only between 30 and 100 US$—with much better image quality. I was just lucky that there were only a few weeks between the market research and the presentation at the trade fair and that a "return" would not have saved anything anyway. And so, together with all our competitors and the brand new digital cameras, we stood on the trade fair stands and were virtually crushed by the demand there. ◀

It doesn't matter whether you commission focus groups with 15 participants or representative studies with several thousand participants to investigate the future viability of an idea: As a rule, you can and should save yourself this budget: Consumers can't imagine the future any better than your marketing team.

▶ People have real difficulty imagining the future and products that have not yet been invented. Even if a product already exists, but is not yet widespread, customer surveys will take you anywhere—just not into the future.

4.5.7 Even the Tiniest Changes Revolutionise a Market

Of course, it would be nice if you could shape your own corporate future by coming up with something as ingenious as the idea of the car, the computer, or the smartphone. But honestly, who can? Most innovations that shape corporate futures tend to be small changes to offerings or more inconspicuous inventions. Just think of the coffee filter: a piece of blotting paper folded on the side—how sad would our breakfast look without this invention?

Example

The company AirBnB, for example, brokers private accommodation. Hundreds of other websites have already dedicated themselves to this business before—with conceivably moderate success. The essential difference between AirBnB and the other, rather futile attempts is that the creators of AirBnB asked themselves why hosts achieve such different success in renting. As a result, they identified the images that hosts were posting on the mediation platform. Many of the images were amateur shots, taken with simple cameras or even cell phones—snapped rather than photographed. AirBnB took an unusual step and offered to send potential hosts a professional photographer,[4] free of charge, to take pictures of the rooms they were renting—the results spoke for themselves: accommodation arranged skyrocketed, sales increased and AirBnB is now one of the biggest competitors to the world's hotel chains—at US$46 billion more valuable than Mariotts, the world's largest hotel chain (Reiche 2019). ◄

And there are numerous other examples. Casio, the Japanese multi-electronics company, lived for many years solely on the insatiable urge of its founder Kazuo Kashio to invent and market new products. As early as the 1980s, the company distinguished itself by launching a new product every second day on average. The company did not rely on market research or one big new product, but on a large number of products that were sometimes only slightly modified by combining two known technologies. For example, the company created calculators and watches with all kinds of special functions, musical instruments, mini televisions, or digital cameras more out of a pure desire for novelty than through Excel-based top-down planning—a horrible idea for many entrepreneurs! But the company continued to develop as a result and still has its finger on the pulse of the times, even though there were always flops among the many new products. But that was just part of the game at Casio.

Unilever also took the path of small solutions when it needed a nozzle to atomize liquid detergent in such a way that it could be turned into powder. Top-down didn't work here either, so they decided to go for evolution instead of revolution: they just started trying. This involved building several variants of the nozzle and then testing which variant was best suited to the task. This was again built and tested in different variants. After 45 improvement cycles, a highly complex nozzle was created that fulfilled the desired task—without anyone being able to explain why this nozzle was so much better (Wolf 2012). Sometimes innovation also requires the desire to play!

► So success is by no means always the result of big, revolutionary ideas that leave everyone speechless with amazement. Most often, it is the small development steps that move companies forward. Evolution instead of revolution.

[4] In 2017, AirBnB then changed this concept: Today, the company only offers the procurement of a professional photographer, who then takes these pictures for a fee (https://www.airbnb.de/professional_photography).

4.5.8 Outsiders: Attacks from the Side

Let us look again at the examples of good and bad future strategies already discussed. There was Olympia, for example, the company that was so firmly convinced that the future of the typewriter was the constantly improved, fully electronic typewriter that it did not even notice the real competition when it was already driving sideways into the company's flank at maximum speed. Or let's take the digital cameras, which were only offered by the classic camera manufacturers when the competitor from electronics was already on the market.

We can currently observe a perfect example looking at the automotive industry: While traditional manufacturers still considered electric vehicles to be science fiction, Tesla—a start-up!—began selling production-ready vehicles that outshone even the best classic cars in terms of driving comfort, acceleration and running costs. But that wasn't all: since none of the suppliers could come up with a suitable offer for a small electric-powered city van, logistics service provider DHL simply bought a start-up called Streetscooter and developed its electric vehicles itself. What's more, as of 2017, DHL also sold these vehicles to third-party companies and had thus also become a competitor for the automotive industry.

I am very sure that your company keeps a constant eye on the competition. However, if you only look at the development of the market in your future scenarios as it is today, you may overlook the industry leader of tomorrow. This will happen even more often in the future, as the topic of software will become more important in the future and simply turn entire business models upside down.

For example, the aforementioned company AirBnB has become the most expensive hotel company in the world with an enterprise value of US$ 46 billion—without owning a single hotel. The taxi industry with Uber or the food delivery services with Lieferando.de in Germany are doing similar things. Both have risen to de facto market leaders in a very short time without ever owning a car or having put a single pizza in the oven—although one could certainly discuss the business practices used in one or the other case.

As the person in charge of a "traditional" company, you might be upset that you can practically only achieve such market positions with software. Facebook, for example, is currently (Forbes 2020) one of the six most valuable companies in the world, even though it only offers a platform that gains value solely through the use of its users and whose software supposedly even fits on a regular USB stick.

Nevertheless: Software will dominate future business life and thus redefine competition in all industries. The good news, however, is that you know this now! Because this will not only allow you to expand your market monitoring and thus take up defensive positions in good time, but you can also check which of your competencies are suitable for attacking completely new markets and industries—those in which you are not yet active today—when developing your future strategy.

However, it is important to think critically about the competencies of one's own company. Newspaper publishers, for example, recognized early on that their competence lies more in producing news than in printing it on paper. Did Olympia's competence lie in producing perfect writing machines or rather in decades of experience around perfect writing? Does the expertise of camera manufacturers lie in producing devices with a very specific form factor, or in their optical and photographic experience? You see:

- At the beginning of the future strategy process, it is worthwhile to clarify to what extent the company's mission/vision statement (if there is one) is still up to date and describes the company and the brand in a current, correct, and honest way.

4.5.9 Competing with yourself

Kodak had it in hand: with an almost unbelievable lead, they had developed the idea of the digital camera and thus the killer product to classic film-based photography—two decades before Japanese companies gave the idea of digital photography a broad breakthrough at Photokina 1996. And yet the concept was only half-heartedly pursued—if at all. This surely had to do with the state of the art, as the sensor, the CCD, was initially miles away from delivering consumer-acceptable image quality at 10,000 pixels. But Kodak would have had the money and knowledge, in addition to the time, to develop marketable cameras from the hardware monster of 1975. But Kodak managers did not want to because they did not like the idea of creating competition for the current business themselves.

From the point of view of a shareholder, one could argue that the decision was the right one, since it had brought the company billions in sales and profits for more than 20 years between the invention of the digital camera in 1995 and the actual launch of the digital market in 1996. On the other hand, it was precisely these investors who had to bear the burden of this decision: Kodak's share price, which was still worth almost US$ 94 in February 1997, has since fallen to well below one dollar. What was once the ninth-largest company in the world is now worth practically nothing compared with its original value of over US$ 30 billion. Would Kodak be more relevant today if management had made a different decision back then and actively developed the digital camera? It's impossible to say for sure. But the company would certainly have had the chance to do so. Above all, Kodak would have been in a position to design and implement all the infrastructure necessary for digital images (such as printing, storing and sharing digital images) and to patent it once again, in addition to what the patent on cameras, and before all its competitors.

The Rügenwalder Mühle is a good example of the possible success: Only 30 months after the start of the project "vegetarian meat products" the turnover share with these products already amounted to 20%—additionally!

► So if you are facing the same situation, don't hesitate!

4.5.10 Once Again: Future Management Never Ends!

When I first conducted a strategy workshop with my team for a customer in the automotive sector, autonomous driving and e-mobility were not yet a topic. Only 2 years later, the first signs were visible that the industry, and thus also our customers, would have to deal with them. Another year later, the VW diesel scandal overturned everything and e-mobility was suddenly within reach.

Wanting to take care of the future of your company or your industry is therefore a never-ending project—you should be clear about this from the outset. Just think back to the event funnel for a moment: the closer you get to a future, the more information you have at your disposal—the narrower the funnel becomes and the more accurate your scenarios for that future can become.

Philip Tetlock puts it this way in his book *Superforecasting* (Tetlock and Gardner 2016, p. 175):

> A forecast that is updated to include the latest available information is closer to the truth than one based on less information.

Even if this may not sound very motivating: If you have hoped up to this point that the topic of the future could be settled with a few nice workshops—bury this hope now! If you want to install a permanent future process in your company, then this process never ends, because from now on you must

- constantly lookout for new ideas that can breathe new life into your brand and business, or mortally wound it—depending on whether you find that idea first or your competitor does.

- watch not only your direct competitors over the long term but also start-ups or companies that operate on the fringes of your market. Pay particular attention to seemingly pointless moves—and ask yourself what hidden strategy could be behind such a move.
- pay special attention to your youngest employees and your youngest customers. Are they doing something you are not? If so, are these early warning signs you should be watching for?

In times of constantly changing markets, your decision for future strategy should not be a short-term commitment—it needs as much continuous attention as, for example, your controlling or your corporate communications.

4.6 Let's Be Frank: Are you the Right Manager for the Job?

I know this question might be a little tricky. But please think for a moment about all the people you have hired, or not hired, in your role as a business leader over the years. People who had—or did not have—a certain skill or mindset that was required for an advertised job. As supervisors, we all realize that there are tasks for which a certain type of person would be beneficial or even mandatory. And even for top tasks, every company works with specialists—the Chief Financial Officer, the Chief Human Resources Officer, the Chief Sales Officer, and so on.

But: Leadership tasks in the company change because the company changes. There is something, I call "life cycle" for companies that require different types of decision-makers in the different phases. Let us take a look at a typical development of a company, a market, a product or a brand (Fig. 4.3):

4.6.1 Phase I: Creative Start-Up

At a very young age, as a start-up, because the business model is right, the company goes through a good initial phase. The team that has built up a company or a division and made it successful has the talent to create a functioning and prosperous company organism from nothing. They have "a knack"—or a nose—for having the right structures ready, for taking the right actions, for launching the right communications. They can "create", means they belong to the group of innovators among the managers.

Life cycles of a company

Life Cycle	I	II	II
Description	Startup	Established company	Change-Process in the market/ End-of-Life
Task	Structures must be built and business opportunities must be seized	Structures (internal, customer network etc.) are expanded and optimized	New Markets need to be developed
Decision matrix	Innovative	Consolidating	Innovative
Budget structure	Investment	Profit maximization	Investment

Fig. 4.3 Life cycle model

4.6.2 Phase II: The Company Is Established

The start-up grows, soon reaches a "never hoped for" size—and then stagnates. The product is no longer new; the first and second-generation customers have been reached and have bought; the start-up phase is over. Now measures have to be taken to ensure lasting success and to establish the former start-up in the market.

Too often this then happens: The former young entrepreneur or the management team intensifies the previous efforts, does everything that has led to success so far with even more energy and perseverance, possibly raises even more capital—and then still fails. Seemingly nothing from the old toolbox still works. The magic of the beginning has somehow faded. The company bumbles along from there—or worse—dies. This phase of disbelief and "trying harder" is a common human phenomenon. A neuroscientist once told me this story about it:

Example

In your company, lock a door that is usually always open and observe how your colleagues deal with this situation. I bet the encounter with the door goes something like this:

- The colleague approaches the door and presses the door handle.
- After it fails to open, as usual, he pauses, then
- presses the door handle down once again three/four times.

Only after this action he turns away and tries to continue his way differently. The colleague (and everyone else too!) does not press the door handle down again, but three or four times.

The background to this is (once again) our brain and the power of the subconscious, because something as mundane as wanting to open a door, of course, first runs in the subconscious—we already talked about it briefly. To want to hand the whole thing over to the conscious mind would, after all, be a waste of energy. The situation learned over many years (door is always open) is valued more highly by the subconscious than the experience just made for the first time (door is locked) and therefore tries to use the automatic solution method. Three times, four times—until the conscious mind takes over the job and says "closed, you idiot. Let's find another solution".

Now what, other than a lot of fun, does this have to do with companies? Well, the business leader of the start-up just outlined has had a good experience over some years. His method of running the company and the decisions he made to do so have been successful. He has always been positively encouraged in his actions so far and has thus learned that this way of working is probably "the right one". He, therefore, denies the option that the fault (i.e., that the company is now no longer celebrating success) could result from his way of working or the decisions made with it. After all, everything has worked with these methods up to now! The colleague seeks the error outside and therefore repeats his actions—again and again with the same solution approaches. Just like the door handle. In this case, the matter is probably quite simple—and above all unfortunately different: The colleague probably does not have the right action and decision patterns for the current life cycle of the company.

The company has reached the phase of consolidation: now the task changes. The task now is to consolidate operations and sales via classic sales processes, expansion of the line-up and regular market communication, and simply grow organically. For an innovator, however, this is a boring business to which he can contribute little with his skills. Quite a few innovators then leave the company—or hand over the reins to a new generation.

And that's a good thing because start-ups or divisions that are newly formed need completely different decision-making priorities than established companies. While innovation and development must be at the center of all decisions, in the beginning, the company (or division) needs a different management team as soon as it has arrived at the consolidation phase of life: While *innovators* are the factor of success in the beginning, the *consolidators* are now needed in the second, established phase, i.e., people who enjoy making an existing organization more efficient to compete for market share with competitors.

4.6.3 Phase III: The Downturn

And this finally brings us to the future, because at some point the "grown-up", established company experiences crises that are once again accompanied by stagnation or even loss of sales. If the causes for this are not in the company itself, but in the market, which is facing possibly radical upheavals, it enters the next phase of its life: By definition, it has reached the end of its life with its current business model.

In this third phase, the priorities change again, because now new approaches must be sought with which the company can be transferred into new times: New products and offers, new distribution channels or even completely new markets.

One of the biggest mistakes in this period is to react to the possibly declining market with Phase II methods. Please recall the examples of Olympia, Polaroid or the camera industry: In all these examples, companies reacted to a market decline by withdrawing instead of looking for the innovations that suited them. Specifically, they simply closed down company offerings that were no longer insufficient demand. The abandonment of compact cameras, the withdrawal from the instant photography business or the break-up of the entire Olympia company was declared to be a strategy. From the point of view of the people acting, this may even have been a valid strategy—because when the companies realized the difficulties of their markets, they were in the second phase, and the corporate leaders tended to be *consolidators* mentally. For someone with this pattern of action and decision-making, the priority is to minimize the negative financial impact of a problem no matter what. Saving money, reforming loss-making areas and making organizations leaner is the right method in the second phase—but not when it comes to investing in planning for the future in changing markets.

But how could the management of a company in the second phase have recognized that the slump in sales was not a temporary problem that could have been countered with the well-known measures? Could the downfall have been avoided in the examples given? This is a bit of a truism because the answer must clearly be yes: After all, there are companies in every industry that even emerge stronger from such a market crisis! However, it would have been necessary for those responsible to be aware of their strengths and weaknesses.

While an *innovator* will eventually withdraw from an area—usually out of sheer boredom—when the business changes to the point where it no longer needs innovation, it requires great foresight for a *consolidator* to recognize when to relinquish steering or at least bring in an additional innovator.

In contrast to the *innovator* in the transition from start-up to a chain company, the *consolidator* does not get a clear indication of the transition to the third phase. After all, the decline in the market could just be a small negative dent. Consider Apple's history for a moment: Steve Jobs'first career at Apple ended in 1985, when the Macintosh was introduced and the company seemed to need stable corporate structures. The company's total of three subsequent CEOs with corporate experience (all more like *consolidators*) consolidated the company but lost their way in the still fast-moving computer market, and Apple became a turnaround case by 1996 at the latest. In 1997 the innovator Jobs took over again and put all his eggs in one basket with completely new themes such as the iPod or the iPhone. Jobs saved the company from certain ruin with innovation strategies.

One of the most decisive skills of a leader in shaping the future is therefore to be aware of one's abilities and limitations and thus to be able to put oneself and employees at the right levers at the right time. Is your strength more in innovation or in organization? Are you passionate about sifting through company processes to make them more efficient and profitable? Or do you rather love thinking outside the box and worrying about the day after tomorrow today? No matter what your preferences are—you just need to know them as accurately as possible to set up your team and thus steer your department or company in the right direction.

Incidentally, there are many treatises and seminars on the subject of role-specific leadership and decision-making processes, almost all of which are based on the archetype theories of the Schweitzer psychiatrist Carl Gustav Jung.[5] An example of this is the model in Fig. 4.4.

[5] If you would like to take a closer look at this - and in particular at your own role - I recommend in particular the management model of the Team Management System by the Australian scientists Charles Margerison and Dick McCann, which is offered in Germany by Team Management Services GmbH (2017), among others.

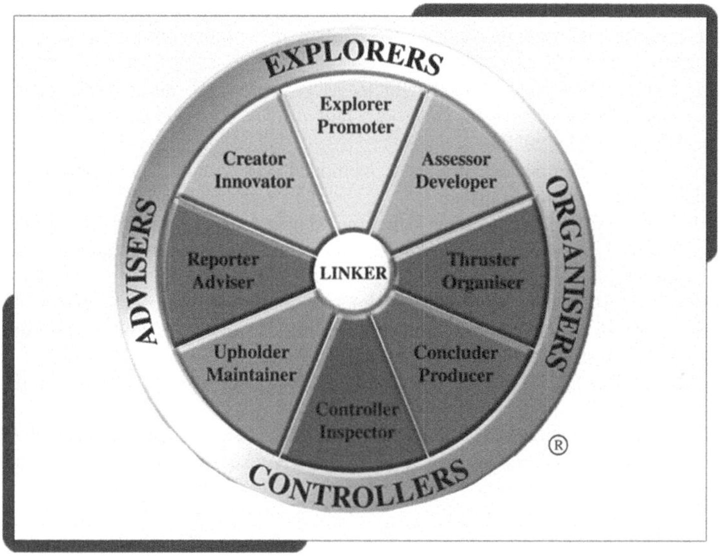

Fig. 4.4 The role model using Margerison-McCann's team management wheel as an example. (Source: The Margerison-McCann Team Management Wheel is a registered trademark. Used with kind permission of TMS Development International Ltd., York/UK. www.tmsdi.com)

Therefore, check exactly which phase your company is in and whether you already have the right resources on board today to prepare well for the next phase. Attempting to lead companies into necessary change processes with the same ways of thinking and working that made them great in the past can only go wrong.

▶ If you run into walls with old methods, you miss the door!

References

Barnekow et al (2006) Soziologie zwischen Produktion und Nutzung von technischen Innovationen. Z Sozialwissenschaften und Berufsprax 29:30–42

Bhattarai RK (2018) Enterprise resiliency in the continuum of change: emerging research and opportunities. IGI Global, Information Science Reference, Hershey

Forbes (2020) GLOBAL 2000 The world's largest public companies. https://www.forbes.com/global2000/. Zugegriffen: 16. Mai 2020

Grundhoff S (2017) Der VW von morgen hat kein Lenkrad und hört aufs Wort. https://www.focus.de/auto/elektroauto/vw-sedric-uber-fluessig_id_6748066.html. Zugegriffen: 20. Mai 2020

Lange L (2011) What Steve Jobs taught us as entrepreneurs. https://www.forbes.com/sites/lizlange/2011/10/17/what-steve-jobs-taught-us-as-entrepreneurs/#678fb209750e. Zugegriffen: 20. Mai 2020

Porter M (2013) Wettbewerbsstrategie: methoden zur Analyse von Branchen und Konkurrenten. Campus, Frankfurt

Reiche L (2019) Airbnb strebt direct listing an. Manager magazin. https://www.manager-magazin.de/finanzen/boerse/airbnb-direct-listing-geplant-bewertung-soll-bei-46-milliarden-liegen-a-1289852.html. Zugegriffen: 16. Mai 2020

Spiegel Online (2015) Porsche-Chef bezeichnet selbstfahrende Autos als "Hype". https://www.spiegel.de/auto/aktuell/porsche-chef-matthias-mueller-bezeichnet-autonomes-fahren-als-hype-a-1052688.html. Zugegriffen: 18. Mai 2020

Tetlock PE, Gardner D (2016) Superforecasting–Die Kunst der richtigen Prognose. Fischer, Frankfurt a. M

Wolf A (2012) Sich durchwursteln: Die Kunst der Improvisation. Z Psychol heute 5:20–25

Wikipedia (2020) Google ads. https://de.wikipedia.org/wiki/Google_Ads. Zugegriffen: 15. Apr 2020

5 Creating your Toolbox for the Future

Abstract

In the context of building strategic future management, you need to apply and combine a wide variety of methods. However, since such tools are not only suitable for future management, you will find the most important creative tools described in more detail in this chapter.

To work with the future, you need tools. Unfortunately, as nobody knows the future, it requires a lot of imagination, fantasy, and creativity. And so you may not be surprised that the tools I will present to you on the following pages are all rather creative tools that can be conducted with pretty little effort. But please don't misunderstand this message: Just because working in "Business Wargames"or the "Google Day" can be somehow fun for employees, it doesn't mean those methods are to be taken any less seriously. The playful aspect only ensures that the participating colleagues drop their previously practiced thinking for the while when entering the workshop and—at least for a short time—break new ground. And that is exactly what working on future strategies is all about!

I would like to make one more remark. My main criteria to select tools is their support for the process to create your company's future strategy development. But many of these tools can also be used without such an overarching concept: You have a new concept for your trade marketing? Test the idea with a business wargame. Do you want to deal with the topic of crisis management for your company more than before? Work out typical crises as scenarios with the scenario technique (more on this in Chap. 8).

H. Hilbig, *Shaping the Future of Your Business*,
https://doi.org/10.1007/978-3-658-35349-0_5

5.1 Research Methods

The Basic Principle

▶ Systematically search instead of "googling". Develop a system for gathering the same set of information over and over again. From the changes in each search run, you will recognize the possible movements of your competitors and your market.

It is probably completely unnecessary to write a "how-to" on researching, right? You type what you want to know into Google and you immediately have the most important results. Is that so? Granted, Google has significantly changed the task of searching for something from the old days when you still had to search for sources in large dark libraries. But has the process of research become easier since then? Probably not, because you will never get *all* the results with a simple search—not to mention, whether your results include what would be most relevant to you. Since Google started sorting results according to what you might like best, i.e. what best matches your previous search behaviour, your location, your preferred language and similar criteria, since then you unfortunately only get filtered information on the front pages.

So let's go through typical research as an example: To do this, let's assume that for your planning, you are looking for all the information you can find about your market, your competitors, future developments and future competitors. Then your most difficult task is, first of all, to put to the back of your mind all the knowledge, experience and personal contacts you have through your long activity in this market: Especially if you have been successful in a market for a long time, you run the risk of having gathered information from tunnel vision so far (see Sect. 2.3, "Olympia"). Even if you share a stable market with let's say the same five competitors, you may *assume* that you know certain information rather than *knowing* it.

I cannot stress this aspect often enough: Unproven assumptions are the biggest danger for any strategy process. In consulting, I created pretty detailed profiles for all major competitors—as well as potential future competitors. Almost all information required for that can be found openly on the web, and it actually only takes the right search technique as well as some experience to create such profiles from it.

One of our clients once wanted to see how well their competitors were staffed with development engineers, how large their share of development costs in sales was, and how these figures had changed over the years. While our client's management was still pondering what kind of business information services they could legally hire for this information, we analyzed the annual financial reports of each competitor and systematically pulled the desired information (along with many others) from there. You wouldn't believe all the information you can find on the net—including information about your company, by the way!

You should spend a lot of energy on this part of the process: Some companies and executives equate the term research with using a search engine. A fatal mistake! As we have already seen in Sect. 1.7, "Big Data"), you get data, not information, from Google & Friends. In addition, a good portion of know-how is also required to successfully deal with Google. The right and important information is not usually found on the first three pages of results. On this topic alone, one could hold all-day seminars or write books.

Nevertheless, I would like to give you four practical tips at this point so that your research will be particularly successful:

5.1.1 Tip 1: Determine What you Want to Find

Before you start researching, create a sort of director's notebook for yourself:

- Which questions would you like to know the exact answers to? You will not always find exactly the answers you want—the Internet is not a structured encyclopedia. But the more precisely you clarify this question beforehand, the closer you will get to the desired result. For example, do you need the number of new vehicles registered each year in an EU country by type? You won't find these numbers in every country. But you might find figures on the country's total vehicle population in a newsletter instead. And by continuously monitoring this source, you can quickly calculate the new registrations …
- What structure would help you compare your competitors well and see changes quickly? Build a KPI structure here for monitoring all competitors. In addition to revenue and profit, perhaps also values such as employee numbers, number of branches, number of products sold, investments in research and development, land ownership, etc. Again, you may not find exact data on every value for every competitor—but you wouldn't believe all the information that is freely available if you just search. Now build an overview chart from all this information along with the sources you are observing and update it regularly, at least once a year. You will gain massive new insights from the observed changes alone, I promise! Your competitor has increased its development budget by 15% in the last few years and is currently hiring new sales reps, but without changing anything in their current product offering? Watch out! He may be planning to introduce a new product group!

5.1.2 Tip 2: Search as you Would Design a Web Page on the Topic

Many people searching for and writing information on the Internet using different terms than professional providers use on websites: Just think about cars. The "official" language will use words such as car, automobile, etc. On blogs and in chats you may see completely different expressions (i.e. "jalopy"). English language Thesaurus mentions up to 8 synonyms—the German language knows up to 14. But for industry insiders and manufacturers, those products are called automobiles, and that's how these products are named on websites. Because webmasters of such B2C (business to consumers) vendors are mostly aware of this topic, they take this into account when planning the so-called keywords, i.e., the search terms that are given to the search engines to help them.

Not so, however, in the B2B (business to business) area or the areas where companies talk about themselves (for example, on pages like "About Us" or "Investor Relations"). There, by no means all websites are structured in such a search-oriented way, and the effort that webmasters put into keyword building in these areas is rather low. But since you depend on exactly such pages for competitive intelligence, you simply turn the tables and search as if you were creating the website yourself.

5.1.3 Tip 3: If you Are Not a Native English Speaker: Search in English Too

Especially if your industry is also international or you also have international competitors, you should look for content on worldwide sites. Even a quarter of a century after the introduction of a commercially usable internet, almost 60% of all websites (and even more of the content) are in English (German: less than 3%!) (W3 Techs 2020) In particular, comments and discussions that can provide you with valuable advice and links are more likely to take place on English sites, purely in terms of numbers—unless you are looking for typical local topics.

Theoretically, Google also displays international results. However, from my experience, I can only recommend to analyse such international search results mainly to see which other interesting search terms you should use to get a bit closer to the desired information. After all, very few of us are so fluent in the English language that we know every synonym. Just think again on the topic of cars we just discussed. In addition, there are a large number of colloquial terms, especially in discussion forums and blogs. And because this is the case in all languages, you can eventually be guided to the “right” search terms for Google by studying found foreign language pages.

5.1.4 Tip 4: Switch Google to English Language Search Results

If you are not a native English speaker, you most probably have set your Google Search to your native language. Google allows you to temporarily switch your search engine to English search results (as of May 2020): To do this, search for any term and find the menu item “Settings” on the right-hand side of the results page below the search window. Please click on this and select “Search settings” again. Under “Languages” you can now choose which results should be displayed in languages other than your native language.

Important: If you normally browse the Internet in your local language, Google usually knows this and will then show you results in your native language. For research, I, therefore, recommend explicitly switching off your native language—this way, you will see English-language results right at the front of your search.

Secondly, you should set the priority of the resulting origin. This is especially important if you suspect that interesting information is published or discussed in a specific region—for example, if your competitors have established their headquarters or a central development there. To do this, select the Search Settings tab and then the regions at the very bottom of the page.

Important: The Checkpoints

Once a year, you should at least get a complete overview of the competitive information. To do this, be sure to arrange fixed checkpoints with the responsible employees, i.e., appointments at which you repeatedly review the information collected over weeks in its entirety. This is the only way to avoid the danger of being surrounded by gurgling water in the mudflats. Do you remember? Many changes in your market are announced only by small and smallest news, which, perceived individually, are easily overlooked and which, considered together, may already send out clear signals. Depending on your industry, it may well be too late if you don't do this triage until the annual strategy meeting—you may find that, without realising it, you already need a lifeboat.

Therefore, in addition to your annual strategy meeting, be sure to schedule at least one additional meeting to review, analyze, and interpret the information you have found so far.

5.2 Google Day

The Basic Principle

- ▶ You encourage your employees' desire for creative, unconventional ways of thinking and working and let them work for a day on a project of their choice—completely detached from normal day-to-day work—with clear rules. In addition to attunement to strategy creation, you may gain completely unexpected ideas.

A great tool to increase the creativity of a process is Google-Day. Strictly speaking, this tool does not explicitly belong in the topic of future management: It can be used whenever an organization or a group of employees is to be introduced to explicitly creative ways of working.

Let's face it: for many companies, having to be creative is by no means part of their daily business—agencies and comedians perhaps excepted. And that's why hardly anything makes less sense than asking employees: Let's be creative now!

On the other hand, when it comes to looking to the future, that's exactly what you need: to think differently. To think outside the box. Being able to imagine things that don't exist today. If you start a workshop without the participants being tuned in to the creative work, you can end up with what I experienced at my first international wargame, which was attended mostly by Japanese managers: Everyone was gathered in the meeting room promptly at half-past eight in the morning (the workshop was supposed to start at nine), sitting at the tables that hadn't been cleared away yet with laptops open in front of them and looking at me expectantly. How do you get a group like this in the mood to break rules and jump mental hurdles—especially cultural ones? If there's one corporate culture where "Let's all get creative now!" doesn't work that way at all, it's certainly Japan's. I have learned a lot from this incident and therefore like to start future workshops with a warm-up phase, which I do not yet include in the actual workshop: Gladly also with Google Day.

Anyone who has had the chance to visit a Google office will be fascinated by so much "unconventionality": When I had an appointment at the office in Hamburg, the football kicker standing next to the reception desk was still the smallest difference to "normal" office spaces. What excited me the most was a conference room, completely looking like a train of the Hamburg's subway. Green meeting oases, swimming pools … if you are now curious, just check out the pictures on the web. But Google not only surrounds its employees with unusual workspaces, but it also encourages their creativity in other ways. Not out of pure humanity, of course:

Google benefits from employees producing new ideas—however crazy they may be. And so there is supposed to be regulation at the search engine giant, according to which every employee can take one day a week off from their normal tasks and devote themselves to a topic chosen by themselves. Google doesn't dictate anything, but in addition to time, it also provides the resources to work on those projects on a small scale. It is all about turning "crazy" ideas into projects, projects into business cases, and finally business cases into products. Many of the things we use every day at Google today are said to have come about in this way.

Now, to start your planned workshop without laptops flipped open and out of the meeting culture experience you've been trained for years, you'll want to take some limits out of the participants. The Google Day is ideally suited for this purpose.

Each of the participants receives a letter a few days before the workshop, preferably signed by a high-ranking company representative. In it, he is attuned to the workshop and receives his instructions for the Google Day. Here is an excerpt of the content—the writing style should of course be adapted to your company.

Example

On the day before the workshop, we ask that you do not work as usual. Please make sure that you are not tempted to work on normal day-to-day business via smartphone, phone or by co-workers. No "just popping into the workplace" please! No matter how important your work is, the future workshop is more important.

Use this day to work on any topic instead. An idea that you have always wanted to pursue. A thought that still lacks concrete. Or even a tangible topic. Take your pick. It doesn't have anything to do with your field of work—you can work on topics from any area of the company. You are also completely free to choose whether you want to do it at your workplace or somewhere else—or from home. You may also team up with a maximum of one other colleague from the workshop participants.

There are only two conditions for this day:

- The topic or project you choose must have something to do with our company in the broadest sense.
- You need to get to the point that day where you can present the results on the next day. ◄

It is important that the scheduled presentation takes place and is conducted appreciatively by the company or project management so that the work of this day does not seem like a "gimmick" to the participants. Whatever happens on that day—your participants have spent a whole day outside their normal way of thinking and will certainly not expect a workshop planned afterward with their laptops open as a normal meeting. And as company management, you will be amazed at how many creative ideas will emerge from this day!

5.3 Framing the Future: Future Scenarios

The Basic Principle

▶ Instead of guessing what the future of your industry might look like (that would be a prediction), you try to create different "probable" pictures of the future—the scenarios—by estimating the most important influencing factors and combining them.

This section deals with the creation of future scenarios, which should in no way be confused with predictions of the future. Future scenarios tell stories from the future that could be created by strictly logical deductions from the present. And this makes it obvious what this part of a workshop is about: you will develop variously credible, logically derived stories that could describe the future environment of your market.

To clarify the difference and also the procedure of creating scenarios, please take a look at the following sentences:

> We will not be able to produce enough crude oil for much longer to be able to run as many cars in the future as we do today. And because battery-powered vehicles will never reach the range of today's cars, 330 million hydrogen-powered cars will be driving through Europe in 20 years.

This is a classic prediction on a specific topic ("the future of the automobile")—even verifiable because the creator even gave a date (20 years from now)—based on four concrete assumptions:

- Oil is becoming scarce.
- E-mobiles will not reach today's car ranges.
- In 20 years, 330 million passenger cars will (still) be driving through Europe
- Hydrogen as a fuel for cars is becoming marketable and attractive.

For the scenario technique, however, we have to granulate these statements even more finely into influencing factors and characteristics:

- **Influencing factors** are the issues outside the own company that could influence the development of the own market. In the above example, these would be the stocks of crude oil, the range of battery-powered vehicles, the vehicle population in Europe, the market maturity and the market attractiveness of hydrogen as a fuel for cars.
- **Characteristics** are the assumed values of these influencing factors, i.e., in the above example: the oil supply will **deteriorate drastically,** battery-powered vehicles will **not improve significantly** in technical terms, the number of passenger cars will **remain** at the current level and hydrogen will become economically and technically **attractive.** A characteristic is, therefore, so to speak, the evaluation of the respective influencing factor.

The sad thing about predictions is that only one assumption doesn't have to come true for the prediction to die an inglorious death. What if battery-powered vehicles do improve significantly in technical terms? What if this prediction simply did not take into account significant influencing factors?

And that's what scenario creation is all about. Let's develop the workshop work step by step:

5.3.1 Step 1: Determine the Influencing Factors

In a workshop, the first step would be to identify all the key factors influencing your market activity. Here, working in small groups as well as the presentation and condensation in the whole group via moderation cards is suitable. When condensing, make sure that the formulation of the influencing factors is concrete and in no way judgmental. For the above example, these could be:

- Availability and price of oil for use in internal combustion engines
- Technical development of e-mobility
- Technical development of autonomous vehicles
- Sharing concepts or car ownership

"Will we even be able to produce enough oil?" on the other hand would be an example of a judgmental phrase. Try to focus on a few, crucial factors. From my experience, four core issues are just manageable.

5.3.2 Step 2: Define the Characteristics

Once the workshop team has agreed on the influencing factors, it goes back to group work to describe a set of characteristics for each influencing factor. Of course, you could describe the oil stocks in five or ten gradations (we have no oil—we have a little oil—we have enough oil—we have a lot of oil, etc.), however, for the sake of simplification, I strongly recommend choosing only two assumptions (high and low) for the expressions. You will be combining these sets later, which will quickly drive up the number of scenarios then. If you were to combine four influencing factors with two assumptions each for the car example above, you would already come up with $2^4 = 16$ scenarios that you would have to check. If you choose three characteristics (good, medium, bad) per influencing factor, you are already at $3^4 = 81$ scenarios!

If you work only with two values, you could have a "conservative" and a "progressive" assumption developed. Each group now defines the characteristics by a descriptive sentence: So not only "we have little oil", but rather "oil is becoming dramatically scarce, price is rising massively". The more concrete these descriptions become, the easier the third step becomes.

After all, groups have completed this task, they present again on the moderation wall, condense and merge. Your result might look like Fig. 5.1.

5.3.3 Step 3: Define Meaningful Scenarios

Now, unfortunately, it becomes a bit formal: Now take all the influencing factors (marked as A, B, C, and D in the table) and "rate" them with one of the two expressions (1 or 2). Then you get a set in the form A1-B1-C1-D1 etc. In total, you would have formed 16 such sets in the above example.

However, not every set makes sense. For example, the combination A2 (oil becomes dramatically scarce and unaffordably expensive) with all conservative manifestations B1, C1, and D1 (everything remains as it is) can be excluded as a scenario, because it is already recognizable that a dramatic change in oil will lead mankind looking much more intensively for other solutions. By the way: I had already written this last sentence in the first edition of this book, long before the pandemic and before the pharmaceutical industry showed what a joint effort of all global forces can achieve in a short time. In the workshop, it would be ideal if you could print out the sets with the contents on large format paper (at least A3 sized) and hang them on a wall. Then, before each combination, let the groups decide for

Einflussfaktoren		Characteristics	
		1: conservative	**2: progressive**
A	**Availability and price of crude oil as basis for combustion engines**	Availability ok, price increases moderately	Oil is becoming dramatically scarcer, prices are rising massively.
B	**Technological development of e-mobility**	Development stays slow, infrastructure, charging time and capacity grow only moderately, cars remain expensive	E-mobility is making a big push. There will be fast-charging stations at every parking lot. One battery charge will be enough for driving 500 km on average and vehicles are becoming cheaper than vehicles with combustion engines.
C	**Technological development of autonomous driving**	Development proceeds only sluggishly	Technology is making great leaps and will function almost flawlessly within a few years
D	**Car sharing instead of car purchase**	Car sharing remains just another, rather small option besides regular rental cars, public transport and individual transport owned vehicles.	Car sharing models become the dominant transportation method and practically a part of public transport

Fig. 5.1 Example table for creating scenarios

themselves, e.g., via sticker ratings, which are the most sensible sets that need to be followed up. Sets that are very unlikely or even pointless should be dropped. The goal is to end up with about four such sets selected for the next step.

5.3.4 Step 4: The Scenarios: Make the Story

Working for future concepts is not rational a lot of assumptions and beliefs will influence your work. But when you are finally finished with your initial work, you need to share it with other members, maybe including the board of directors, who did not join in the workshop. For this reason, the task now is to write story for each of the (four) sets that makes it clear to those non-participants what kind of world we might find ourselves in. These stories (with the descriptions of influencing factors and characteristics behind them) are the "future scenarios" we are looking for, a quasi-glimpse into the future. Describe what will move people in each of the assumed sets. What might happen if this scenario occurs? Any consideration is conceivable as long as it is a logical consequence of the previously defined assumptions.

Whether you let the groups write these stories—or only note down keywords that are then elaborated outside the workshop depends only on the structure of your workshop. The following examples could be results of the groups—the first two still in keywords, the third example already in a partially elaborated variant, which could thus already serve as a basis for a management presentation and further planning.

Example

- **Scenario 1: Evolution of individual transport (A1-B1-C1-D1)**
  Individual transport continues to develop evolutionarily. New technologies such as e-drives or autonomous driving are only slowly conquering the market. The existing players have time to familiarize themselves with the new technologies. Success in the market is defined by one's actions and competitive activities.
- **Scenario 2: Revolution through e-mobility (A1 or A2-B2-C1-D1)**
  E-mobility and autonomous driving technologies are developing and spreading rapidly. Existing players may be at great risk because the new technologies require less specialist knowledge. And the necessary knowledge of battery technologies or electronic vehicle control is not part of the core competence of today's car manufacturors. The demand for electricity and internet capacity will increase abruptly, leading to a massive surge in demand for renewable energy. The still mainly mechanical automotive workshop sector will suffer substantial losses because there are significantly fewer wear parts in e-cars. Instead, there will be a radically higher demand for electronics specialists, which existing workshops will not be able to access. Vehicles will be repaired and serviced "online" more often. Massive impact on oil companies. The sharp drop in the value of existing vehicles, as even used models with combustion engines, hardly find a market (especially in the case of variant A2).
- **Scenario 3: Market disruption (A1 or A2-B2-C2-D2)**
  - The market changes as a result of e-mobility, as in scenario 2. In addition: autonomous driving dramatically reduces traffic accidents, which has a massive impact on the 40% (see GDV 2019) of insurance companies that have motor vehicle insurances as their core business now. Traffic jams will be eliminated as long as only automated vehicles use the roads. Due to the recognizable economic benefits, "driving vehicles yourself" is made unattractive by the legislator through corresponding tax burdens, which further accelerates the change from self-driven to autonomous vehicles.

- Autonomous driving makes it irrelevant whether a vehicle looks attractive, how it drives or what performance data it has. Instead, the focus is shifting to interior design and what passengers can do in the vehicle while driving. The equipment with entertainment, communication, work and rest facilities becomes the most important selection criterion. Being able to choose individual equipment depending on the occasion makes renting vehicles more interesting than buying them. Car sharing will overcome the taxi business and become extremely inexpensive because acquisition and operating costs are significantly lower than with today's taxis due to the elimination of human drivers. Through the online connection to bus and train schedules (which will also run autonomously), the self-driving individual vehicle will develop into a feeder for public transport. At the same time, most private vehicles will no longer be needed and thus no parking spaces will be required.
- Due to the elimination of parking spaces and because electronic vehicles can drive more closely timed in road traffic without producing traffic jams, road sizes can also be radically reduced in metropolitan areas. The follow-up costs for road construction are reduced dramatically.
- In view of the many obvious advantages, these new transport systems are being promoted and conventional, self-driving vehicles are gradually being penalised by taxation and finally even restricted by bans.
- The rapid change creates a drastic problem for a few years with disposing of end-of-life vehicles with combustion engines (close to 400 million passenger cars in Europe alone), for which there is no longer any demand anywhere. An intelligent vehicle recycling industry emerges, which has a life spam of just a couple of years.
- Since loading batteries requires different infrastructure and will cause people to change their usage behaviour, regular gas stations will disappear from the market to the same extent as vehicles with combustion engines do. Reduction of gas stations will raise opportunities for new tiny 24/7 shops to secure local supply outside of regular shop opening hours.
- Car parks in cities are no longer needed and are either being dismantled, rededicated or closed.
- And so on and so on and so on … ◀

Could this be the basis for a story with which you can expand the way of thinking in your company? Are there enough approaches for business models in it, even if your company were a provider in the traditional automotive sector today?

Just be sure to remember that this story must never stand alone, but must always be one of four or five scenarios. Otherwise, it becomes just a prediction again. With (for example) four scenarios, you are virtually describing a field in which the future is likely to occur. That is why we call this method "Framing the Future".

I would also like to make a few important comments on scenarios and predictions:

Scenario Precision

Predictions are impossible in principle because they are supposed to describe what will happen. And as we have seen, it is possible to be right at best by pure chance. However, a prediction that is hardly more correct than by chance is a very poor basis for your entrepreneurial actions, isn't it? Even the inventor of the scenario technique,[1] Pierre Wack (Wack 1985), a manager at Royal Dutch Shell, warned against relying on a single prediction in times when the future changes daily. That would not work. Instead, he introduced the modified method of scenario description at Shell as early as the 1960s. In contrast to predictions, which describe what *will* happen, scenarios are supposed to describe what *could* happen. They

> … describe assumed sequences of future events and are based on the combination of various external influencing factors and driving forces about whose future development there is a high degree of uncertainty. Scenarios represent various possible manifestations of the future. (Recklies 2001)

However: scenarios remain unspecific. And even the ones you create might not turn out to be real. But that's not the point, because, in the end, you should get a feeling for which divergent developments in your market you should be prepared for.

Could more be achieved, more concrete and tangible results be obtained, if this tool was carried out in four, eight or a hundred iterations in the context of a workshop instead of two? I tend to think not. Okay, I have never tried designing a workshop over a whole week—interesting thought—but no! The reason for this opinion, apart from the capacity of the moderator and the preparation required for this, is mainly the problem of motivation. Once you have spent two

---

[1] Strictly speaking, Pierre Wack is not really the inventor. He has further developed a technique that goes back to Herman Kahn, who introduced it in the RAND Corporation, an institute for futurology founded by the American Department of Defense, in the form of military simulation games. However, no one is as often named as the successful founder of this method as Wack.

days running creative workshops with a hard-working group, interest and concentration wane: Another group session—oh, please don't! Don't pin moderation cards again! The playful element is lost from the workshop and you lose the creative impulses.

Software-Based Future Scenarios?

A tool I strongly recommend *not* to use are software-based future scenarios in workshops. However, this does exist: Management consultants offer to use special software to record the boundary conditions for the scenarios, define mathematical relationships between them and then calculating the future like KPIs.

Feel free to leave such approaches to the large corporations that can provide enough money and manpower for such number-fixated solutions. I reject such systems myself outright because on the one hand the fun factor and thus the creativity of such methods are completely lost. More importantly, however, these calculations suggest a bogus accuracy of results that is pseudoscientific and thus unhelpful. Imagine (simplified) that your workshop was able to establish a mathematical relationship between oil availability and the price of gasoline at the pump, and you calculated gasoline prices ranging from 2.67 US$ to 4.01 US$. After 5 years, someone looks at the real gasoline prices, which are at 1.50 US$, and realizes that you were completely wrong with the scenarios you developed. And now? Was all the work therefore worth nothing, just because some figures were not accurate? Wasn't it for your company more important to describe and prepare for scenarios rather than estimating the figures on the gas prices?

When searching for your market future, refrain from using such strictly formal methods, which often simply reflect management's desire for Excel spreadsheets. In any case, such quantitative approaches cannot describe your future any better than qualitative methodology.

Even if "storytelling" doesn't fit with the Excel and PowerPoint-based reality of management today: Stick to finding the approaches to stories you want to tell with the scenarios in the workshops and work them out in the aftermath of the workshop. Remember what Pierre Wack said. Scenarios are there to expand the options in the minds of senior management. And Shell should know, after all, right?

5.4 Business Wargame

The Basic Principle

- ▶ With a group of employees as heterogeneous as possible, you play out the reactions of various stakeholders to market or strategy changes.

A wargame is a kind of interactive role-playing game and is designed to enable participants to identify completely with the role they are playing. This role could be competitors, but also—depending on the market situation—customers, traders, authorities, legislators or non-governmental organisations. It is important for the success of this element that you can put the participants into a playful competitive mode. Only then will the participants start fighting with each other for market share, just like in real life.

By the way: Even if the focus in this book is on the future process, wargames are suitable for very different strategy checks. Participants can not only check their actions but also find creative solutions to them.

Example

One of my wargames was to optimize the operational processes of a new product area that was slowly growing up. Due to the rapid growth of the division, processes, communication channels and decision-making processes had not been developed quickly enough and there was a crisis at all ends. Frustration spread throughout the Asian headquarters, the European headquarters and the more than 30 branch offices across the continent. In a wargame, we re-enacted this situation with colleagues from the European headquarters. The moderators acted as a disruptive factor, constantly intervening in the game with new requests, for example, about "production problems" or as dealers, customers or journalists asking for more information. Communication between the groups took place via "e-mails" (moderation cards, each of which was pinned to a pinboard representing a mailbox), which, as in real life, had to be answered quickly. We virtually played out the day's business in fast motion with the different people involved. This game started quite stiff but was fueled by increasingly fast-paced interactions. At some point, the participants lost their shyness and played their roles well. The breathlessness increased and grew to exhaustion. The problems that also occurred in real life—overwork, a lack of understanding of the ever-changing demands of each other's groups, and dissatisfaction with the sometimes less than concrete responses from headquarters—became apparent in the game. But also the essential cause—lack of understanding for the role, the abilities and the limits of the possibilities of the other parties—could be identified and positively changed by subsequent modules of the workshop. ◀

In a future workshop, the wargame has the task of incorporating the fundamental way of thinking of other market participants into the future considerations and, if there are already concrete strategy approaches, subject these to an initial check. With the results of a wargame you really have the chance to anticipate possible reactions of the market at an early stage and thus to adapt your strategy accordingly.

Which "Roles" Should Participate?
It's obvious: The competition! Watch out! This question is not quite so simple. For one thing, only a limited number of stakeholders (four to five at the most) should be represented for a workshop, because otherwise, a creative, successful and result-rich workshop will quickly turn into a tough training mass. On the other hand, your competitors are usually not so different that it would be worthwhile to "bring" them all to this workshop. Therefore, we usually form several clusters of similarly structured competitors, from which we then include one representative competitor in the workshop.

Who Will Take Part in the Workshop?
Your employees. But who exactly? Jim Collins, the US author who in the 90s examined large companies to see whether they had a common success factor (see Collins 1994), once described a workshop concept with which companies can address the topic of vision and mission. To select the participants, he defined the so-called Mars Group (Collins 2002). The goal was to find people who should imagine that they could now start their company on Mars and make it successful. Unfortunately, the rocket only had limited capacities, which is why not everyone could be taken along and therefore had to be selected. The goal is not necessarily to put the company's commanders, chiefs and heads in the rocket, but to take the people with you that you need to ideally be able to mirror your company on Mars—with all its strengths and positive characteristics.

I liked this description so much that I suggest this selection to our clients for every workshop. So it's about finding a group of creative and engaged minds that represent a cross-section of your company. And it shouldn't matter whether the person is part of the inner management circle or not. A workshop that includes participants who have only been delegated there by virtue of office or rank will fail. Please keep in mind that the primary goal of the business wargame is to "anticipate" the reactions of your competitors as best as possible. The more diverse and colorful the group of participants, the more promising the results will be.

One question that is always asked is whether or not outsiders should participate in such a workshop. I cannot give you any conclusive advice on this, but I would like to share some thoughts with you:

- In this workshop, you may discuss and work on very intimate details of your company strategy. If you are thinking about external participants, consider whether these details can be released to the eligible participants or whether they can handle them. I would have little doubt about this with a notary or your physician, who are already bound to silence by virtue of their office. On the other hand, the question may arise as to what notaries and personal physicians can contribute to a creative workshop. But what about other suppliers who may—now or later—also accept mandates from your competitors? You can hardly ask them to forget all the insights they gain in your workshop, when they accept a call from one of your competitors.
- You should also bear in mind that external partners such as agencies or management consultants always have their agenda that can influence your workshop—service providers are also entrepreneurs and want to sell something. There is nothing wrong with that in itself, because that is the business concept of the respective external partner. On the other hand, a service provider who knows the company well can help to balance out the tunnel vision that has already been mentioned several times. So weigh up: If the supplier can detach himself from his own agenda for the workshop, such external voices are definitely enriching.
- Finally, there are situations in which external know-how can be helpful to the result. Think, for example, of an automotive brand that wants to review the strategy of a car of the future. Experts from the battery industry, environmental associations or even your Ministry of Economics can provide absolutely valuable input.

So should you involve external people in the workshop? Well, the Englishman would probably say: "It all depends …".

How Large Must/Could the Group of Participants Be?

The absolute minimum number of participants that you need to represent a stakeholder, is certainly three: trying to initiate a creative process with two people would already be challenging. Then you will need to represent at least three stakeholders plus the representatives of your own company, which brings us to the absolute minimum number of participants of twelve people. How does it look upwards? More than five stakeholders in the workshop make the processes boring and in each stakeholder group, five participants are ideal. Beyond that, it tends to get difficult again. Let us therefore formulate as a goal that one should have at least twelve, but at most 25 participants for a wargame.

The "Script"
In an ideal world, the business wargame could take place spontaneously: The participants usually know the company, the products and the competitors. But who lives in an ideal world? So you need a kind of framework story, which you can best describe in a script. However, only you have the complete version. For your participants, you work out excerpts of the respective role that the colleagues are to take on. Add general information about the market you are dealing with (only clear facts, no interpretations!), as well as possible pre-researched overviews. Of course, you can also have the teams do such research themselves during the workshop, but if you like to have my advise: Don't do that. Teams may get lost in the research task and you may miss other important results simply due to lack of time.

Now let's look at the structure of two role scripts using the aforementioned semi-fictional example. I refer to your own company as "the host" in order to differentiate it from the competing companies.

Example

1. **Host role**

General market briefing: You are a supplier of lawnmowers with a somewhat smaller market share. The market is overall stable and has had an equally distributed market share structure for years, led by two dominant market leaders. The market volume is essentially divided between two strictly separate groups of customers who opt for either electric or petrol engine mowers. Other technologies, in particular, hand mowers, cordless mowers, ride-on mowers and robotic lawnmowers tend to play a minor role in terms of volume.

From market research you know that there are a large number of garden owners who welcome the idea of robotic mowers, but do not want to leave such expensive products (purchase prices from 800 EUR) running unattended day and night in the garden. In addition, the problem of the remaining lawn cuttings is unsolved for these customers.

Strategic move: Through cooperation with an e-mobility provider, you are planning to launch a completely new robotic mowing system on the market that is equipped with extremely powerful motors in order to reduce the running time to a few hours per week. In contrast to existing mowing robots, the function of autonomous driving is controlled by a so-called teach-in phase: after driving once along the outer limits of the mowing paths with this robot, the robot has memorized this route and will drive inside of it from now on. As a very positive side effect, a much better lawn appearance can be achieved. The robot is also capable of emptying the grass cuttings independently at a specified location.

With this product segment, you want to attack the long-standing market leadership of the two large competitors, whose economic basis is the conventional mowing products.

Information on the host role: <Here follow facts and figures that may be relevant to the workshop>.

Information on competitor role 1, 2, or 3 Information: <Here follows information for each competitor or group of competitors, as well as pre-researched content.>

2. **Competitor role**

General market briefing: You are one of the two market leaders in the lawnmower segment. The market volume is essentially divided between two strictly separate groups of customers who opt for either electric or petrol engine mowers. Other technologies, in particular hand mowers, cordless mowers, ride-on mowers and robotic lawnmowers play a rather minor role in terms of volume.

Strategic move: A smaller competitor is planning to launch a completely new mowing system that combines the advantages of previous lawn mowers with those of a robotic mower. The new system is characterized by the fact that it can autonomously mow even large gardens within two hours, is electrically powered, produces extremely little noise—thus can also be used on Sundays—and can even dispose of the lawn cuttings independently. This new product category is seen by your technicians and salespeople as capable of making a lasting attack on their own business. A patent search is still underway, but an initial review has revealed that your company cannot simply offer identical concepts at this time.

Information on competitor role 1, 2 or 3: <here follows information for each competitor or group of competitors as well as pre-researched content>.

Information on the role of all other player teams: <Here follow facts and figures that may be relevant to the workshop.>.

These are only rough examples of the structure of such scripts, from which, however, some of the research required beforehand is already apparent.

By the way, you don't have to think in 60-page prose works at all if you have the scripts in mind. The whole thing becomes more exciting if you compile quasi scrapbooks, i.e., books with collected newspaper clippings, links to websites, etc. because this gives the whole thing a real competitive character for the participants.

You don't have to collect all the information from your research (as was necessary in the past), because your teams should have laptops with them in the workshop so that they can do their research. It is therefore sufficient, for example, if you provide a link to a, particularly successful Google search.

> The more professionally you prepare this part of the workshop, the greater the participants' acceptance of the process and their own results. If the scripts then look professional, you increase the fun factor of the colleagues immensely!

The Workshop Procedure

A business wargame is conducted in two to three iterative loops. If you haven't already done so, form groups, each representing the host company, key competitors, and/or other stakeholders. Make absolutely sure that your groups are heterogeneous (not all product managers in one group!) so that assessments can be looked at from as many different angles as possible. All groups receive the same briefing about the host company's planned change in strategy and then retreat to different war rooms, i.e., the headquarters of the respective competitors.

Tip

Try to give the groups as playful an introduction to the wargame as possible by decorating the rooms and other staff (T-shirts in company colours and with competitors' logos). There are no limits to your imagination. This may sound a bit silly to typically serious companies. But: The more your teams are in playful competition mode, the better and more accurate the results of your game will be! Remember, that's exactly why the fun meeting rooms at Google exist.

Iteration 1 (Duration Incl. Presentation 2 to 3 Hours)

So the teams leave to their "headquarters" and now have to answer two sets of questions in a first-round:

(a) *Who are we? What distinguishes us? How are we mentally structured as an organization? What resources do we have? What is our view of the market?*

With the questions of this set, the groups should develop an internal view of the represented competitor or stakeholder: If VW looks at Opel as VW, this gives a different picture than if Opel would describe itself. With this exercise, we want to try to get as close as possible to the internal view of the competitor. How do they tick? How does the market looks to them? What pleases, what annoys the competitor's employees? Only when the group has answered the first set, the second part is worked on.

(b) *What does the host company's planned change in strategy mean for the represented group? What countermeasures, based on the resources available and the mentality described, will the competitor take?*

With these issues, there are two groups for which there must be adjustments: First, there is the host company. Most of the time, you will nominate your own team for this (which, by the way, should then be the only one to stay in the big room for psychological reasons—has the "home right"). However, I have also played wargames in which all employees alternately played the roles of competitors and the host company. Obviously, depending on the starting point chosen, you need adjustments to these questions here. However, the host company should also answer questions (a): There are said to be companies in which beautifully formulated guiding principles on the intranet or in a picture frame in the executive office do not fully reflect the company reality … On the other hand, other stakeholders, such as consumers in-demand markets, naturally also need slightly modified rules of the game, since they are more concerned with estimating reactions than with countermeasures. Here you need to create meaningful, individual instructions for your script.

Trust that you will find the right combinations for each set-up! After about two hours have elapsed, all the groups come back together, take off their roles and first present the answers to questions (a) (who do you represent) one after the other. In each case, the panel discusses them (if necessary) and gives feedback to the group for the second round. Afterwards, the groups again present the developed counterstrategies one after the other, so that at the end a picture emerges of what would probably happen in this market if the original strategy plan were implemented.

The following step is one of the most important of the wargame. You should definitely take your time and only do it if your teams are still fresh enough. If they are not, postpone this part until the next day.

Counterstrategy (Duration: Approximately 3.5 Hours)

For the following process, the teams figuratively put on the caps of the host company again (or put on the T-shirts for real) and now put themselves in the position of knowing the reactions of the market and the competitors to the original strategy. All teams now put themselves in the role of the host company and discuss the following questions in small groups:

- Does it make sense to go through with the original strategy unchanged?
- If not, what do we change?

Invite the groups to think of everything and to have every resource of the company at their disposal. Allow them to think in terms of products as well as measures. The only exception: Proposals that only work through endless budgets (always popular: a huge marketing campaign that crushes all competitors) are taboo as long as they are not accompanied by qualitative proposals (for example: "we need the money to explain the advantage vehicles having roofs to every cyclist in a guerrilla marketing campaign").

However, each group should limit itself to only one, in its opinion, most promising approach. New products *or* sales strategies *or* a new marketing approach *or* ... Make use of the variety of different suggestions you will receive.

After the time has expired, the participants meet again in the forum and present the proposals. If the discussion leads to the conclusion that the strategy planned so far (alone) will not be sufficient, a recommendation should also be made as to which of the measures discussed is the most promising.

Iteration 2 (Duration Incl. Presentation 2 Hour)

Finally, think through the task in a second iteration: In a final act of the wargame, the participants put on the competition shirts again and take on the role of competitors: through a 'leakage', i.e., a non-authorized publication in the press, you have learned about the revised plans of the host company. What does this mean for you and your company? How will you react to it?

Here, too, the results are compiled in the forum after about an hour and discussed if necessary. All results of the three runs (i.e., Iteration 1, counter-strategy and Iteration 2) should be well documented and handed over to the company management after the workshop. They represent the ideal starting point for real planning!

5.5 The Strategy Diagram

The Basic Principle

- By creating an activity matrix of your competitor, you can identify their weak points and develop strategies to target those very weak points.

Developing strategies seems to be real rocket science, which only a few "master brains" ever have mastered: If you search for the term "advertising" on Amazon Germany, you will find over 50,000 results in the books category—under the search term "strategy development" there are just 343 (as of April 22, 2020). If you associate strategy development with almost genius, world-changing concepts, you won't find it in those 343 books either, unfortunately. The good news, however, is that in most markets, it feels like 90% of all successful strategies are based on systematic analysis and then selectively applied measures. And this is exactly what the almost trivial tool does that I would now like to recommend to you: the strategy diagram. In just five steps, you can create a plan at the end of which you can read off the measures you should take.

5.5.1 Step 1: Who Is your Competitor?

Against whom is the planned strategy directed? This may sound a bit harsh and bellicose, but such formulations are necessary if we want to talk about effective strategies. Think of chess for a moment—here, too, strategies must be chosen according to which is your next target: the rook, the knight or even the queen of your playing partner.

The simplest answer to this question might be, "Competitor? That's every other vendor in the market!" But beware—unfortunately, the strategy game is not that simple. Under no circumstances should you focus on every market player at the same time. The top four reasons are:

- **Reason 1: Market maturity**—you don't have an immediate opponent in the short term.
- The mature market has existed for so long that competition is thriving. The market is based on demand, means customers can—and do—choose from a variety of different offers. The counterpart to this is an offer-based market, in which there is a limited supply in terms of quantity or quality. The customer who is willing to buy has to choose between a limited selection. Examples of this are the top tier of smartphones (in 2020: Samsung S20 or rather iPhone 12) or the early days of good old delivery services (Domino's, Smiley's or picking up the pizza yourself from the Italian restaurant around the corner?). Typical offer markets can therefore be found in the early days of a new industry or product category, as well as quite often in the area of consumer electronics that are in particularly high demand. If your market is still in this phase of life, there is simply no point in devising strategies to conquer or displace the market—you will only burn money unnecessarily! Instead, work on being the first supplier who can also satisfy the demand. And what you need for this is a sufficient quantity of high-quality goods.

- **Reason 2: Your resources—**you simply can't be everywhere.
- So let's assume from here on that you need a strategy for a demand-based market that is served by at least five—rather more, of course—companies. In such a market, the main focus is usually on market displacement. Do you keep a constant eye on all competitors, do you respond to price fluctuations of all five? Do you react in every country and every distribution channel as soon as one of the five makes a move there? Of course not—no company can sustain that. In fact, in my experience, this is one of the main reasons for ineffective business strategies: Actions and tactics are deployed with a watering can instead of being developed with a focus on just a few competitors. Budgets and resources are wasted instead of consolidated. And in the end, the whole beautiful strategy fizzles out because the strength is simply not there to take on every competitor in every market segment.
- **Reason 3: Your market position—**defend or attack?
- So far clear: You are in the demand-based market and are now focusing your strategy on pushing a few competitors aside. Now, where you stand in the market is quite essential: If you are #1 in the market, your natural first market opponent is #2—and your strategy must be defensive. You need to defend your first place against the second. But if you are number 2, you need two strategies: On the one hand, you need to attack the market leader—your goal is market leadership—so you need an attack strategy. On the other hand, you need to fend off the market third, so you need a defensive strategy.

If you are a newcomer to the market or can be classified as "far from it", your market activities must be completely different again.

- **Reason 4: The unknown—**sharpen your all-around vision!
- We already talked about this case and the examples from Sect. 2.1 shows how dangerous it is to focus "only" on the known competitors. When the electronics company Casio threatened to shake up the photo market with its first digital cameras, the leading camera manufacturers developed a defensive strategy that could only hit an outside competitor. Since it was by no means clear at the beginning of the market whether these products were more of a camera or an electronic product, success depended on the choice of distribution channel: electronics stores had all the prerequisites to be able to demonstrate the advantages of the "electronic camera"—it was just that the major camera manufacturers did not have access to this market. Photo retailers, on the other hand, were

perfectly capable of handling these products from a photographic point of view, but (in the mid-90s) had absolutely no understanding of PCs and electronic products. So the traditional photo industry invested, opened the door to the digital world for photo retailers at enormous expense, and thus kept the external aggressor Casio out of the market. So your strategy needs to include your closest competitors and, if you're a market leader, keep an eye on outside vendors as well.

5.5.2 Step 2: The Activity Mindmap

Now we start with the strategy diagram. In Fig. 5.2 you can see an anonymized example. The similarity to mind maps is of course absolutely no coincidence because that is exactly the goal.

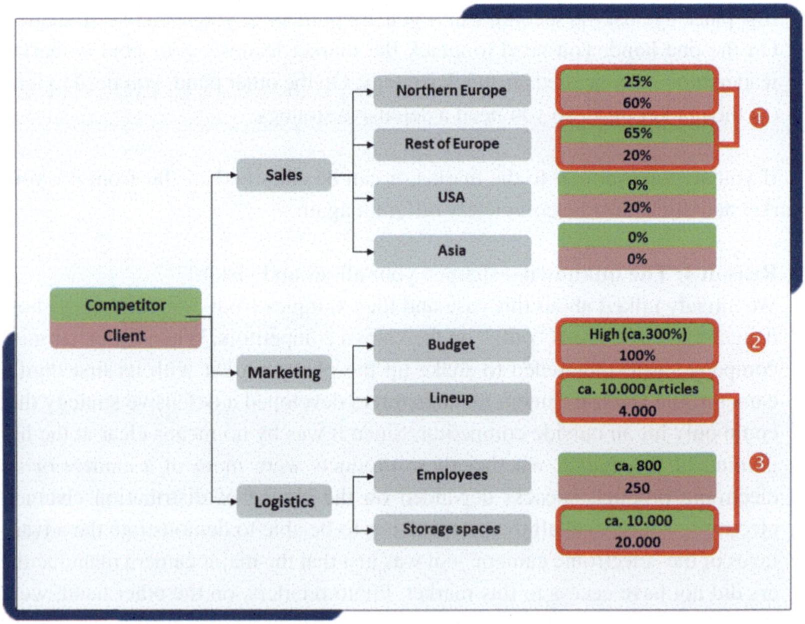

Fig. 5.2 Strategy diagram

Create a mind map[2] of all your competitor's activities, for example, with the following questions:

(a) Distribution:
  - In which geographic countries does your competitor operate?
  - Where does it operate directly with its branches, with independent distributors?
  - Which distribution channels does it use?

(b) Product offering:
  - How is its product offering structured?
  - Is he a full-line distributor or does he only offer some of your market's products?
  - If you are active in a market with a range of articles numbering in the thousands (e.g., stationery, car parts, DIY): How many articles does the range include?

(c) Marketing:
  - Which channels does the competitor use?
  - How active is he in the trade?

This is really only a small example. The list of questions you can and should ask is usually longer and—most importantly—needs to be answered on a market-specific basis. For example, one of my clients brought the competitor's stock size into play. We'll take a closer look at why this can be useful in a moment.

5.5.3 Step 3: Scope of Activities

Now your market knowledge is in demand—if you do not have concrete data available through good research, estimate shares and scope of activities. For the sales of an internationally active competitor, it could look like this: How much sales does he make in the USA, how much in Asia, how much in Europe? And how much in Germany (or DACH—depending on how you are organized)? For marketing: How much does he spend on trade marketing? How much for classic advertising? In which types of media? Does he do PR? Himself or via agencies?

---

[2] If you are not yet familiar with the mind map tool, you can find a short introduction here: https://de.wikipedia.org/wiki/Mindmap.

You don't know the numbers? No problem. Guess! Because in the end, it doesn't matter if your competitor makes a true 12.78% or an estimated 20% of its sales in the U.S.—it's the smaller part of its business either way. If that sales is then done via a distributor rather than an own branch, then it's pretty probable that your competitor won't launch an attack there as quickly as he might in his core sales region with own branches. And he might not react as quickly there.

The more details of your competitor's activities you concretely estimate, the greater the overview you gain. And the easier it is to find weaknesses—and thus points of attack for a strategy.

5.5.4 Step 4: Add your Own company's Values to the Strategy Diagram

To arrive at an effective strategy, now add to this diagram the values that describe your own business.

▶ **Important**
If you want to analyse several competitors because, for example, as the number 2 in the market, you need both an attack and a defense strategy, create a diagram for each competitor.

Because your competitors are usually not identically active, these diagrams can look completely different: Your biggest opponent is a foreign company, active worldwide, but with a clear weakness in Germany? In this case, it is important to look at sales shares in the various continents. Your second competitor is only active in Germany, but is the market leader here—in this case, it is probably less about countries and sales and more about distribution in Germany, marketing, etc.

5.5.5 Step 5: Strategy Development

I have to say one thing up front: I am not a fan of overbidding strategies. When Volkswagen boasted a little over 10 years ago that it had carried out the largest outdoor advertising campaign in Germany ever, Toyota spent an estimated EUR 40 million a little later on carrying out that this was *really* the very largest outdoor advertising campaign in Germany ever. The object of desire was the launch of a small car called the Auris, which—analysed in retrospect—did not sell any better than any small car launch before or since (Hilbig 2013). Overbidding strategies have two major drawbacks: Spending even more and appearing even stronger somewhere simply costs significantly more and is therefore always a finite pleasure—because neither you nor your competitors have endless budgets. And secondly, this "more" is rarely justified by correspondingly larger sales, as the Toyota example shows.

I have always been attracted to strategies that target competitive weaknesses or even unexplored terrain in a market. The strategy diagram tool is ideal for this, because it shows at a glance where there are significant differences between you and your competitor. And it is precisely these differences that you need to proactively exploit for your own benefit. Please take a look at the reduced[3] diagram in Fig. 5.2, which we used during the peak of the Corona crisis to develop a market displacement strategy for one of our clients for the period after the lockdown.

The competitor (green) has its main business in other European countries, where our client (red) was not yet so present. Compared to our client, the competitor spent a lot of money on trade marketing and had a significantly smaller warehouse despite a larger product range. An approach for a post-Corona strategy could now be derived from each of these points:

- **Point of attack 1: Focus of sales in other European countries**
  At the time of strategy development, it was foreseeable that Germany had the chance to emerge from the Corona crisis earlier and less weakened than many other European countries. We used the strength of our client in Germany to signal to the customers there at an early stage that our client was fully capable of acting and delivering throughout the crisis. As the market was time-critical, the immediate delivery capability was a clear competitive advantage. The client used this strength and the time advantage in the home market to make attractive re-entry offers to dealers in the rest of Europe as well—always with reference to the strong delivery capability.
- **Attack point 2: Extensive, expensive trade marketing**
  The client's market is a typical B2B market. Besides the presence at trade fairs, trade marketing is by far the most expensive form of marketing in such a market. The competitor had therefore built up its marketing with very expensive methods. The customer, in turn, used the time of the shutdown in Europe to reach out in (otherwise) hard-to-reach ways. Over many months, multipliers

[3] For the sake of clarity, the diagram is reduced only to the most relevant points for the example. The original map was of course much more complex.

and potential cooperation partners were sought in the social networks, who reviewed products of the market anyway. And for a fraction of the cost of elaborate trade marketing, the client will be able to provide credible recommendations for its customers in the future.

- **Attack point 3: Small warehouse space with a huge line-up**
  The competitor had set up his business pretty perfectly for just-in-time deliveries. Through continuous procurement, it was able to keep its inventory small in normal times, despite a large supply of items, and thus keep its costs low. The supply chain failure during the Corona phase—especially from China—suggested that the company would be slow to return to full supply capability after the shutdown. We, therefore, recommended that the company stock up its own warehouse as far as possible and signal early on to all dealers, but especially to the competitor's dealers, that it was fully able to deliver.

Three differences in the strategy diagram could be used for an attack strategy on three levels.

Perhaps you are now asking yourself whether this is not too simple a thought. Can you really develop market strategies that easily? "That can't work..." Is that what you're thinking right now? Then let me tell you now a closely guarded secret of the guild of business strategists: It's actually that simple! Take another look at Chap. 3, with the (mis)success secrets. As a rule, there were really only one or two points of attack that the respective protagonists used (or unfortunately missed). My colleagues and I do not work in any other way. We analyse the market situation, look for the competitors' weak points ... and you know the rest now. Good luck!

5.6 Tactical Prioritisation

The Basic Principle

▶ Once the future scenarios and the associated strategies have been developed, it's a question of which measures do you adapt first? Quite clearly: the most important ones! With the principle of tactical prioritization and a relevance analysis, your B2B customers, dealers or employees tell you what you should start with.

Don't worry, it won't be scientific, even if the title of this chapter suggests it. What we are dealing with here is a pragmatic way of finding out from your customers what is really important. Because in fact, the question of which measures to take when it comes to the goal of "improving your market position" in general is significantly underestimated in terms of its importance. Take a quick count: How many advertising media or points of contact do you have with your customers in marketing alone? Website, newsletter, product brochures, direct mail, social platforms… you're bound to have 20 to 30 activities, aren't you? And now please add all the activities that influence the relationship with your dealers and customers from other areas of the company: In Sales, this could be the pricing structure, the frequency of visits, the professional competence and the friendliness of the sales colleagues. In order processing, for example, the availability, the competence of the employees on the phone, in training the relevance of the topics or the frequency of training appointments, and so on.

So you quickly come up with up to three-digit numbers of measures that need to be considered. And each one shapes the relationship with your customers, dealers and employees—sometimes more, sometimes less. On the other hand, no company has the financial and human resources to deal with all the issues at once. So it's a matter of deciding what to do first: the website has been criticized by your customers? So renew that first? But what if the website plays virtually no role in the success of your business? What if your customers know about it, but never use it and don't base their buying decision on the website at all?

So before you can evaluate which of your actions are well or less well received by your customers, you need an analysis of the relevance that each action has for your customers. Only the combination of "important" and "good"—from the relevance of the action and its evaluation by your customer—then results in a concrete plan of what you should change.

Now, you can't simply ask customers which measures are most relevant to them. The question "How competent do you find our hotline staff on a scale of 1 to 10?" yields a disastrous result if the respondent was disproportionately annoyed with the customer service just last week. However, this may still not change his willingness to buy because there are entirely different factors at play here. Knowing the relevance of each measure is therefore highly important if you want to develop a well-founded tactical plan of action.

For all stakeholders with whom a long-standing relationship exists—such as B2B customers, dealers or even employees—this relevance can be determined wonderfully via a customer survey with correlation analysis. In three steps, you practically get a "roadmap" for the priority of tactical measures:

5.6.1 Step 1: Identification of Contact Points/Measures

In a first workshop, you gather representatives from all company divisions with (direct or indirect) customer contact and have them create a kind of mind map of which contacts your customers have with the company and which measures affect them. It is important to create this analysis separately for each customer group, because in the end you may only ask customers about contact points they have. If you provide training or POS material for a certain dealer group, but not for another, you should not even ask the question.

Important

Make time for it! I once conducted this first workshop with a software customer, who at first couldn't see why we were scheduling such a large group of employees for a whole working day. In the end, the event actually lasted eight hours because we had lengthy discussions about supposedly clear points such as "people to approach" or the customer structure: every division of the company had its own ideas on these points—without these ever having been discussed across departments beforehand.

5.6.2 Step 2: The Customer Survey

Next, conduct a customer survey. This can be done via an online survey tool and—in very simplified terms—determines the customer's rating for each touchpoint. Control questions for the question clusters (marketing, sales, order processing, etc.) complement this survey.

5.6.3 Step 3: The Statistical Evaluation

In the end, it is a matter of calculating a correlation from the content-related evaluation of the generic terms and the details. For example, it is determined how the values from all the marketing tools queried correlate with the overall evaluation for marketing. Unlike the first five parts of this chapter (Sects. 4.5.5 to 5.5), there is little point in going into the exact "how" of this method in more detail—unless you have statistical expertise and an appropriate analysis program (such as IBM's SPSS) at your disposal. In general, you will probably need external assistance. The good news, however, is that such relevant analyses are available as ready-made service packages. An example of this is shown in Fig. 5.3.

Fig. 5.3 Relevance analysis on the topic of marketing. (Courtesy of © united communications GmbH [2020]. All Rights Reserved https://www.united-channel-insights.de/)

So even if you can't implement everything with onboard resources in this case, I would like to recommend this tool to you, because it provides clear decision support for executives—especially management—in the question of where resources would be most sensibly deployed across departments for further market conquest.

▶ **Another Tip**

Such tools can be used not only in strategic future management, but also wherever the aim is simply to improve current activities. The only restriction is that only markets are surveyed in which the respondent and questioner have a regular business relationship. In addition to B2B markets, these could also be all direct trading partners or even employees (employer branding).

References

Collins J (2002) Creating the Mars group and beyond. http://www.jimcollins.com/pdf/Mars_Group.pdf. Zugegriffen: 20. Mai 2020

Collins J (1994) Built to last: successful habits of visionary companies. Essentials, Harper Business

Hilbig (2013) Marketing ist eine Wissenschaft–und die Erde ist eine Scheibe. Spinger Gabler, Wiesbaden

GDV (2019) Versicherungsunternehmen nach Sparten. http://www.gdv.de/zahlen-fakten/branchendaten/versicherer/#versicherungsunternehmen-nach-sparten. Zugegriffen: 20. September 2020

Recklies D (2001) Arbeit mit Szenarien. http://www.themanagement.de/pdf/SZENARIO.PDF. Zugegriffen: 20. September 2020

W3Techs (2020) Usage statistics of content languages for websites. https://w3techs.com/technologies/overview/content_language. Zugegriffen: 20. Mai 2020

Wack P (1985) Scenarios: uncharted waters ahead https://hbr.org/1985/09/scenarios-uncharted-waters-ahead. Zugegriffen: 20. Mai 2020

6 Planning the Process

Abstract

Strategies for future business must be regularly reviewed and updated. This requires a systematic approach to identifying the right and important data from the market environment, making credible assessments of future developments, developing strategies on this basis and subjecting them to a stress test before activation. This chapter describes how to do this. Keep in mind, however, that you can detect many small changes in the market only through regular review. So in addition to these tools, you also need continuity for the process.

Future? Attending one or two seminars with speakers, listening to their exciting theses, then an internal workshop—that's how a few new ideas will find their way into the organization. There are said to be companies whose future management looks like this. Even a German business magazine headlines on its special issue "Innovation" in July 2017: *How to create more turnover with new ideas* (Impulse 2017). Sorry, but that can't work! You may have a little success with new ideas now.

But: Sustainable future strategies look different.

Planning for the Future is not a One-off Event

Anyone who looked at the question of trends in personal communication in 1990 concluded that they were well served by (landline) telephones and faxes. In 2000 it was the mobile phone and e-mails, in 2010 the smartphone and WhatsApp, in 2020 the Coronavirus has made video conferencing from the home office popular—and what we will be communicating within 2030, no one knows as of today. A one-time

H. Hilbig, *Shaping the Future of Your Business*,
https://doi.org/10.1007/978-3-658-35349-0_6

workshop allows a good look into the future as we see it today. Tomorrow, however, this future will look different again—I can predict that much for sure!

There is no question that seminars and workshops are good tools too, as Albert Einstein put it, let your thoughts take a different direction. To get things started. But one-off, perhaps even spectacular events such as a future workshop harbour the danger of "getting out of mind quickly": Companies start the future process with great verve and commitment, only to fall back into the previous rut of day-to-day business shortly after the salutary workshop. Please don't get me wrong: day-to-day business pays your salary—so there's nothing wrong with that. However, if you want to deal with the future of your own business in good time, you have to keep at it.

Now, international corporations may have the opportunity to permanently provide resources and people and to be able to recognize and react to possible future developments at an early stage—medium-sized companies with 50 to 500 employees generally do not have this opportunity. But should you just sit back and let the future come? Certainly not!

In recent years, I have therefore combined several effective tools that I have used in a wide variety of situations in companies into a process that we have now successfully implemented for customers with 50 or more employees (Fig. 6.1). You have already become acquainted with most of the tools in Sect. 4.5.4. Now it is a question of building a rounded process from these. You will find a proposal for this on the following pages. If you want to use this process for your company, please check critically whether you need to make any adjustments.

The basic principle of future management is repetition, i.e., the idea that one must regularly check installed measures and the assumptions leading to them:

a) Has anything changed in your market since the last round?
b) If so, how does this change affect the future scenarios developed?
c) How do strategies need to be adapted to fit the modified future scenarios?
d) How will the market and competitors react to these modified strategies?

The structure may remind you of typical PDCA cycles[1] but puts much more emphasis than traditional impact circles on the P, the plan. So let's start with the research.

[1] PDCA = Plan Do Check Act, https://de.wikipedia.org/wiki/Demingkreis

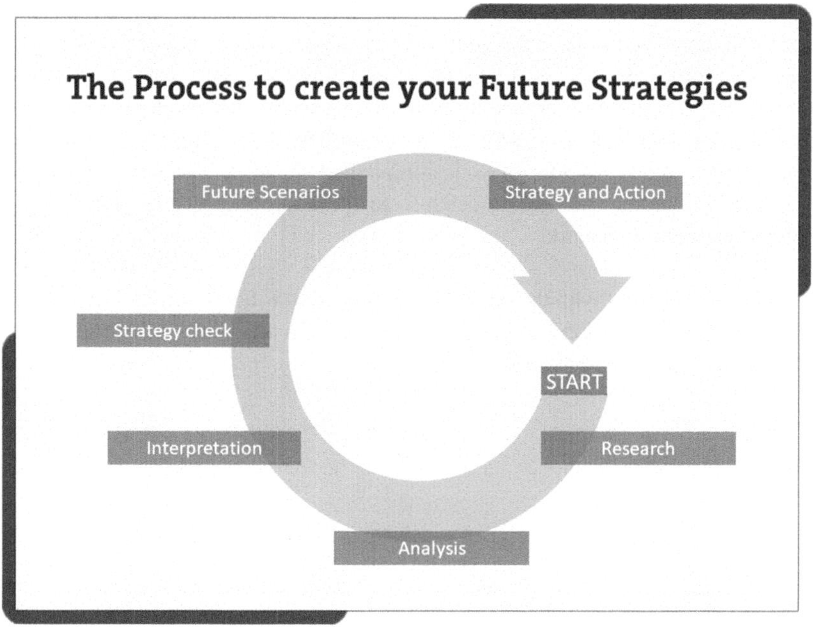

Fig. 6.1 The process of future management

6.1 Research

Who Does?

When you start this process—in the first year—this step will probably be done by the workshop organizer. Once the process is established, you have a loose team that does all the future management tasks. Don't worry: You don't have to hire anyone to do this. Most of the tasks of this process can be done by a flexible team. Just make sure there is a "driver" who regularly calls this team together and communicates results.

What's Happening?

In this step, you gather all the information you need about your market, your competitors, future developments, and future competitors for the next steps. It is important to establish a systematic way of searching for information (see Sect. 5.1). Wild "googling" leads to unstructured data from which you cannot recognize one thing above all: whether you have thought of the most important points. Only when you have determined that, for example, the number of employees, distribution structures or budgets that your competitors spend on research and development are important KPIs and then systematically research these accordingly, you will get a reasonably complete picture of your competitive situation. The little things that you then find on the side, the by-catch so to speak, are then just the icing on the cake of your research work.

▶ Before you start with the detailed planning of your future process, first invest energy and time in careful research. I already said it: You will be amazed at what you will find!

6.2 Analysis

Who Does?
Initially the organizer of the workshop. After the process has been established, the future management team.

What's Happening?
In your research, look for the information you want bias avoiding to early interpretations or filters. Data is data and only becomes information through analysis. You should not take this step too early—and you or your team should not even interpret the collected data (the third step, see Sect. 6.3).

Research, analysis, interpretation? If this sounds too much like an academic dispute instead of a pragmatic approach, the following example might help:

Example

One of my clients, a unique company in the leisure industry, had an ideal source of data for business development: They captured the zip code for each visitor and combined it with a well-intentioned mix of socio-demographic information based on the type of ticket purchased.

Now they added up the postcode data obtained for rural and urban districts, superimposed a map over the sums and analysed them. The finding was seemingly trivial: the closer someone lived to the company's location, the more likely they were to use the company's offer: Hamburg residents (where the company was headquartered) were most likely to use the offer, then residents of the surrounding area, and so on. And even within Hamburg, residents of the district where the company was based made up the largest proportion of visitors. The analysis thus resulted in boring statistics from which no added value could be drawn for the development of sales and marketing measures. So, although the statistics continued to be collected to obtain comparative values on the timeline, there was little momentum in the survey. ◀

Here the data—number of visitors per postcode—was already analysed, summarised into district clusters and interpreted ("this statistic doesn't help us") before the research had even begun, if you leave aside the recording of the visitors themselves.

When planning sales and marketing measures, you should know as much as possible about your buyers and their purchase decision motivation. The team at the customer had simply not taken this research step, and so analyses could only deliver meaningless results. In addition, the data, which was very finely granulated, had been unnecessarily grouped into large clusters right at the beginning of the process, thus destroying valuable information: In the city of Hamburg alone, there are over 100 city districts and postal codes. However, the customer's analysis only used the city's seven boroughs.

We researched further data, such as the socio-demographics of the respective neighbourhoods belonging to the individual postcodes, which we then combined with the visitor statistics and came up with results that completely contradicted the client's previous assumptions:

- The apparent residential proximity as a factor turned out to be a statistical error: The borough in which the company was located was simply the one with most inhabitants. So it wasn't that many people came from here because they had a short commute, but simply because it had the most people living there.
- An examination of affinity—number of visitors per 1000 inhabitants—showed that this borough around the customer location was by no means particularly affine. Rather, people with large numbers of children from city districts in the other boroughs had chosen to visit with above-average frequency and had also accepted long journeys to do so.
- Finally, we were even able to make predictions about visitor numbers depending on periods of bad weather by comparing them with weather data.

Unfortunately, there are always companies that place a higher value on quick results than intensive engagement with what appears to be a familiar market. Hence my suggestion:

▶ Even though the result of the analysis should be as condensed as possible, simplify your source data as late as possible. Any data condensation destroys information, which may prevent you from seeing correlations.

6.3 Interpretation

Who Does?
The organizer of the workshop, possibly with the support of your marketing department. After the process has been established, the future management team.

What's Happening?
As we have seen, it is best to interpret the results as late as possible. If time allows, you can even leave this to the workshop group. Because it is not only information that is processed there, but, as we will see, strategies are also designed.

Now, what exactly is an interpretation of the data found? For example, if your competitor has kept R&D costs high over the last three years while sales have fallen, you could draw very different conclusions:

a) Has the competitor deliberately not adjusted its cost structure in R&D in recent years because they are counting on an upcoming strategic innovation and need the know-how of their employees for this?
b) Or have they possibly not adjusted the structure because it is not possible to dismiss highly specialized employees so quickly?
c) Or is the reason why they did not reduce the R&D department, because it is one of the most important factors for a (planned) entry into a completely different industry?

You see the same data three times, but three different interpretations, which would inevitably result in different counter-strategies in the following process. Interpretation requires an overview of the entire situation, and misinterpreted data has already cost quite a few companies their success.

▶ If you can, leave the interpretation of such data to your future project team.

6.4 Reaction Test: Strategy Check

Who Does?
In terms of time, we have arrived at one of the elements that should take place in the central workshop. In Sect. 5.4 I introduced you to the Mars Group—the people who would be participating in the workshop.

What's Happening?
Thinking about future developments and developing your corporate strategy based on them is like throwing a stone into water: The fact that you implement a (new) strategy inevitably leads to reactions from other market participants such as competitors, customers, retailers, the press or, in very specific cases, even legislators and authorities. The more important your role currently is in your industry, the greater the reactions will be.

Especially when it comes to long-term strategies for the future, such market reactions should be taken into account as far as possible. However, you can't knock on your competitors' doors and ask them what they think of your thoughts on the future and how they intend to respond to them. But there are indeed ways to approach this topic—even just based on your knowledge of your competitors—quite accurately. The means to do this is the *Business Wargame,* which you learned about in the tools in Sect. 5.4.

The good thing about this tool is that it can be applied to any planned strategic move, and in my experience this allows you to anticipate and factor in possible countermoves quite reliably. In this respect:

▶ Business Wargames are excellent tools for any kind of strategy check—not only for the future process!

6.5 Future Scenarios

Who Does?
The workshop participants. Later, your future team works out the first scenarios ready for presentation.

What's Happening?
Only when all the previous steps have been done do we get down to the nitty-gritty—the future. Since I also described this step in the tools Sect. 5.3, we'll limit ourselves here to a little philosophy—or science fiction—as you like.

Anyone who has ever read corresponding books with the what-if stories or seen film adaptations is certainly familiar with the philosophical approach of infinite possibilities: at every moment we make decisions that could also have turned out differently: left or right, buy or not buy, talk or keep quiet. And with every decision, without knowing it, we have committed ourselves to a multitude of consequences that, if at all, are usually only recognized in retrospect in their full implications.

This is, if you like, the philosophical background to the event funnel that we have already talked about. And since this funnel is also responsible for the fact that *any* attempt to predict a future with certainty is doomed to failure at the outset, we do not even try, but use a trick. Namely, we create a whole series of predictions and thus describe a whole series of "futures".

If one cleverly selects and develops these various options, one has, in the end, determined something like corner flags of a football field: Through these four flags, a field is spanned in which the ball (=the future) will presumably be located during a game. This is what is meant by the "framing "of the future. More about the concrete implementation … well, you know (see Sect. 5.3).

▶ Be sure to give creative elements such as the scenario technique or the business wargame enough space in your workshop. Creativity cannot be forced in such workshops by tight schedules. If in doubt, your workshop will take longer than planned…

6.6 Strategy Development & Action

Who Does?
The Future Management Team.

What's Happening?
The two process steps just described (business wargame and development of future scenarios) take place in a future workshop that will pull your best experts out of their normal work process for about two to three days, depending on the task at hand, and will put no small strain on them. At the end of such a marathon, in my

experience, the team reaches a stadium of "creative exhaustion". Colleagues are, if you'll pardon the expression, simply done by 5 pm on the third day. So if you have rough future scenarios in hand at 5 pm, you have achieved the goal of the workshop. If you even have initial strategy approaches, then you are far ahead of schedule.

From now on, you should hand over the further tasks to a small, internal team that develops a proper strategy paper based on the results of the workshop. Then, the action begins you've learned a lot about the possible future during the process, you probably have between three and five scenarios in front of you, and now you need to take action. This doesn't necessarily mean that the day after the workshop you make the big investment in i.e. refocusing your research just because a future scenario says you won't be able to make a difference in ten years with current knowledge. But you should start proactively putting out feelers:

a) Is there any evidence that any of your existing competitors are already showing a similar focus?
b) Has anyone in your industry been looking for researchers with specific skills in job ads lately?
c) Are there cooperation agreements between universities and your competitors?

Look for any change in the market that can support or bring down the scenarios you have developed—confirm the fundamentals of your strategy!

Even if your research today yields nothing in this direction, establish a regular search methodology so that you can notice changes as quickly as possible: Get regular updates on key topics from Google and their programmable search agents, sign up for interesting newsletters or paid press clips—stay on the ball. Keep Casio's success in mind! And important:

► Put this at the top of your research list when you repeat the process next year!

References

Impulse (2017) Impulse kompakt: Innovation. https://shop.impulse.de/impulse-kompakt-nr-5.html. Zugegriffen: 20. Mai 2020

Designing the Initial Workshop 7

Abstract

In this chapter, we look at how to assemble the different insights and tools into a well-rounded workshop concept. Not every market always needs all the tools suggested. Adaptations to your situation are not only allowed but necessary. However, keep in mind that you should always plan the process leading to your future strategy as a whole—avoid "cherry-picking"! Developing future strategies without, for example, having defined scenarios in advance for which these strategies are to apply, makes just as little sense as, for example, evaluating markets without having researched them in advance.

In the whole process around the development of good future strategies, the workshop represents a kind of emotional highlight. Here, creative approaches and hopefully hints for solutions emerge. A good workshop motivates. Because the role of the workshop is so central, I go into detail about this tool and have even dedicated this separate chapter to it.

I have encountered companies where the term *workshop* reflexively conjured up images of 20 people sitting at a table with coffee and biscuits, laptops open, and highly concentrated on comparing the results of various Excel lists. Please don't. Workshops in the future process must first achieve one thing: they must foster creativity and combine it with the company's expertise to create innovative approaches. The following instructions are intended to give you an overview of how to prepare and set up such a creative workshop.

H. Hilbig, *Shaping the Future of Your Business*,
https://doi.org/10.1007/978-3-658-35349-0_7

Using a semi-fictitious example that is a mixture of different real cases, we will look at the steps you can take to arrive at initial future scenarios and a strategic approach. What I will drop are detailed descriptions of classic workshop techniques—I assume that if you want to tackle this topic, you have experience as a workshop facilitator. Moreover, there are numerous books and authors on such techniques! However, if you have no relevant experience, I recommend seeking the support of a skilled facilitator: Usually lasting 2 or 3 days at the most, this workshop is not an easy project.

Let us now begin by looking at the structure and timing (Fig. 7.1).

The two most important elements of your workshop are the wargame and the development of future scenarios. The description of these two tools can be found in Sect. 4.5.4. In addition, there is preparatory research before and evaluation after the workshop. The most important step, however, because it is the first step, is the preliminary information.

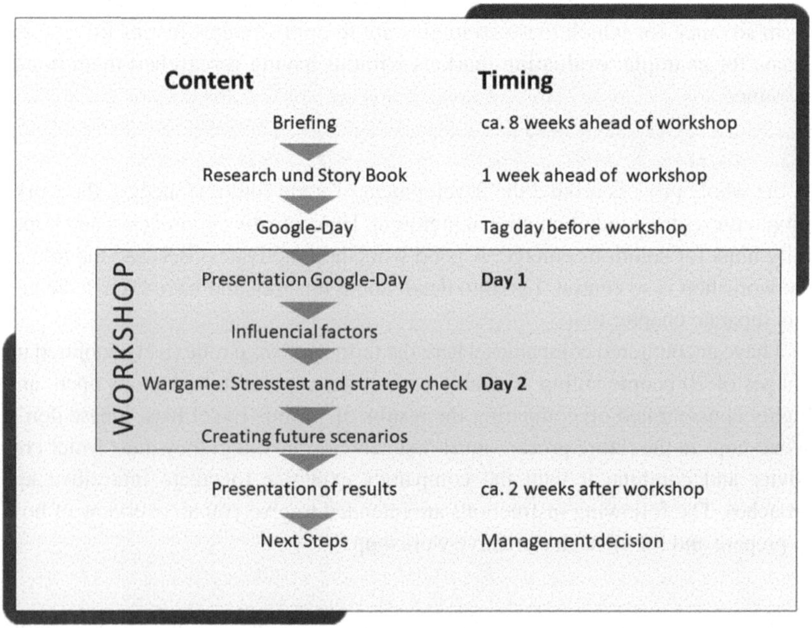

Fig. 7.1 The time sequence of a typical future process

7.1 The Briefing

At the beginning of every measure stands, as always, the briefing. This will be an easy task for you if there is someone who is a sponsor or client for this process in your company: just ask them! It becomes more complex if you had the idea yourself and now have to implement it yourself too. In this case, I advise a co-facilitator who has to critically scrutinize all your steps. Nothing is as dangerous as being the client and the facilitator at the same time, because then you are always subconsciously working towards the goal during the preparation and the implementation. Do you remember pattern recognition? It starts to work here too. You run the risk, for example, of judging the relevance of information already at the selection stage, during the following research and thus steering the workshop in a one-sided way. Apart from the fact that you limit the range of possible insights of your workshop and give away unexpected options, workshop participants may perceive this unconscious control and become ungracious with their moderator. And please, believe me, there is nothing you would like less than to have such a discussion in the middle of the workshop. Therefore my advice: Prepare this process best in pairs and check yourself and the procedure again and again for neutrality.

So now let's move on to the briefing. Ideally, you should ask your client the following questions:

Questions for the Client of the Workshop

1. **Which market situation do you have: Demand or supply market?**
   We have already discussed the importance of this question in detail in Sect. 4.5.9.
2. **Which conditions for change are to be checked on a mandatory basis?**
   After more than 100 pages of dealing with future management, you are probably aware by now that the Future Workshop can by no means provide a blanket answer to the generic question "What should I do?". We need one or more initial assumptions—the primal changes to the market equilibrium, so to speak. In the case of strategic review within a supply market, things are simple: you need to know this new strategy or product concept. In the case of the demand market, you need to define at least one changing framework. This could be:
   - For a company in the media industry: What are the implications of people's cross-media information gathering for daily newspapers?
   - For car manufacturers: What impact will battery-powered vehicles, self-driving cars or car-sharing have on the motor vehicle business model?

- For photo technology providers, how does the photography offering in general change when smartphones themselves are eventually replaced by new technology?

Of course, you can also define several or more complex framework conditions for a workshop. If you even know scenarios that are most likely to occur—see automotive example before—you should consider all of them.

3. **For what time frame should the workshop work?**

   Be sure to remember the event funnel: the more framework conditions you look at, the wider the range of possible outcomes. And the further into the future you look, the more the funnel opens up as well. So if you want to examine ten framework conditions and look just as many years into the future, your workshop participants will have a great time but will dismiss the whole thing as science fiction in the course of the process. So be sure to stay realistic and don't model scenarios that span more than 5 years for your first workshop.

4. **Do you have all the facts now?**

   It may sound a little strange to ask this question in a briefing—do it anyway! Future workshops can fail in many ways—also because the relevant points were not talked about. Such missing information naturally comes from not asking—hence this point on the list—but also gladly because individual parts of the company do not want to talk about it (yet).

Let's fantasize a little: You are planning a future workshop because your company is preparing the launch for a flying car? Great, what beautiful scenarios can be imagined there! But unfortunately, the information was not allowed to be passed on yet, that the technicians only talk about flight heights up to 10 cm above ground as well as speeds up to 150 km/h. So instead of a real flying car, we are talking about a vehicle that floats along the roads rather than rolling on car tires—the strategic product advantage is reduced to a minimum by these limitations in speed and flight altitude. You see, your workshop would be completely nonsensical without this crucial information. You would have thought up and evaluated completely different scenarios than those resulting from the actual planned vehicle.

If you leave out the flying car thing—the rest is unfortunately all too often reality: Sensational products that can change the future of the company have a limitation exactly at the crucial new feature or need a software/app that only runs on one platform (alternatively Windows/Mac/Android/iPhone). Even more common: you are supposed to bring a revolutionary product to life, but your plan fails because production capacities are designed way too small from the beginning, and—unfortunately—you can't change that either. Therefore, make sure you have all the information for your workshop—and that there are no blind spots that people in your company don't like or are not allowed to talk about. If you brief incorrectly or incompletely at the beginning, you won't be able to develop a meaningful strategy for the future at the end.

7.2 The Preliminary Research and the Oetkers' Egg

Almost done! Before it comes to the workshop itself, you as the organizer only have to take one more step: You need to research the future scenarios in advance. To do this, put yourself in the position of a workshop participant who has been given the task of working out the future scenarios and ask yourself three questions that you will also ask in the workshop:

- Which factors are crucial for the development of your industry—which has the greatest influence on shaping your company's future?
- What information about these relevant factors might be important?
- Where can one find such facts?

This step is primarily about making the participants' work as efficient as possible, but without influencing or anticipating results.

So when you work out the three questions, be sure to remain neutral. You should also be sure to pursue and research approaches that you think, include "not very likely" or even "wrong" results. If your preselected information misses such results, the workshop may be misleading—and thus the results may even make no sense any longer. This exercise aims to find a list of sources for each influencing factor that the participants can use to evaluate the scenarios. You compile the results in such a way that you create a separate document with the possible sources for each influencing factor.

▶ **Important**

Leave room for the "egg": There are always rumours about Dr. Oetker's baking mixes that the acceptance of these ready-mixes could be increased by the fact that the user (in the original it is still called politically incorrectly: housewife!) had to add an egg. This small "own" contribution would have given consumers the feeling of having baked the cake themselves.

Therefore, give your workshop participants only research approaches—and thus the opportunity to research details themselves. If, for example, you had identified the number of cars in i.e. Germany as a factor influencing the automotive industry, your research will lead you to the page of the Federal Motor Transport Authority, which you could offer the participants directly as a source. However, since this page appears quite high up on Google as soon as you enter "motor vehicle inventory" as a search term, it would be better to just provide the link to this Google search. In this trivial example—not every factor can be researched so easily—it would even be possible to give nothing at all, because the search term "Vehicle stock "is so obvious that your participants will enter it first anyway.

But (somehow there is a perceived "but" everywhere!): Please do not underestimate this preliminary research and give it your full attention. For many influencing factors for future scenarios, there is only little freely accessible data material, often very hidden, so that you have to think and try a few times before you find it. Under the time pressure of the workshop, teams may therefore fail to find such information and then come to the wrong conclusions—or even leave the workshop frustrated.

With this preparation, you not only help the participants but also ensure that the workshop is a success in terms of both the result and the experience.

7.3 The Workshop

On the following pages, we will go through a workshop together, as it would take place or has similarly taken place. Please understand this list only as a hint, not as a fixed script: The times, the contents, and the processes can naturally change and even look completely different than described here—depending on the circumstances you want to develop.

If you want to introduce a Google Tag, the morning of the first day would be the ideal time to have the results presented. This will put the participants in a "creative mood".

Google Day
Content Results of the Google Day.

Method
Individual presentations with feedback rounds.

Duration
approx. Three hours incl. Coffee break.

Procedure

After a round of introductions and the usual explanations of how the workshop works, all participants present the results of Google Day. The results are documented via moderation cards or flipcharts.

After each presentation, there is a short feedback round in which additional ideas, connections with other presentations, or even links to existing projects are gathered. These comments are also documented in the results. At the end of all presentations, the plenary will once again review all presentations and comment on them. The participants should also evaluate whether individual ideas should be pursued further and presented to the company management.

However, you mustn't approach this part of the workshop with too much expectation. It should primarily serve to set the mood for the creative work that we need for the coming parts. Useful, further usable results of the Google Day may arise—but that is not the ultimate goal!

Scenario Technique

Content Scenario technique—external influencing factors.

Method

Group work with mind maps.

Duration

Approximately 45 min (total requirement approximately 90 min).

Procedure

The next step is to define the external influencing factors for future scenarios. For this purpose, the business model for which the scenarios are to be created is first defined in individual groups—if this was not specified in the briefing. Then the external influencing factors (Which factors influence this business model?) are searched for and noted in a mind map. Then the same happens again with the consequential factors (What changes in the market and for the people if our business model changes?).

For a supplier in the automotive sector, this could be, for example:

(a) Possible business models:
  - Construction and sale of automobiles
  - Production and distribution of automotive parts
  - Services (workshop/maintenance etc.) for motor vehicles
(b) External factors that influence the business model:

- Oil reserves, cost of oil, environmental debate, technology advances in batteries, technology advances in autonomous vehicles, changes in the "social value" of cars (how important is it for people owning a car? Sharing instead of buying), etc.

(c) Consequential effects that are influenced by the business model:
- Insurance market (because autonomous vehicles are much safer to drive than driven by humans).
- Solar panels (because battery-powered vehicles massively increase the demand for electricity)
- Real estate market (because the switch to rented vehicles means that millions of parking spaces for private cars are no longer needed and space is used differently) etc.

Of course, these are only incomplete lists, which must be adjusted on a case-by-case basis. For this purpose, dependencies of such factors should already be presented (for example, oil price depends on available stocks).

The results are presented in groups in the forum, discussed and combined by the moderator into an overall view. This view becomes the basis for the next steps.

Wargame
Content Business Wargame (market reaction test).

Method
Group work.

Duration
Approximately three hours for two iterations.

Procedure
The business wargame process is described in detail in Sect. 4.5.4. At this point, this tool could be useful if your company has a future strategy that needs to be reviewed or even wants to change its strategy. In this case, you can check whether this strategy would survive in your market, taking into account the influencing and consequential factors.

An alternative is to first work out the future scenarios (next step) and only then review the current strategy under the future conditions. Which path you take is therefore determined by your current situation.

Future Scenarios
Content: Scenario development.

Method
Group work.

Duration
Approximately four hours.

Procedure
Now we come to the future scenarios. Here, it will be a matter of mapping conceivable future developments that influence the company's business field, irrespective of the company's actions. The starting point is the results of the wargame, in which we had transferred practically the current market situation unchanged into the future. Everything in our market remained as it was—changes were only to occur through changes in the actions of market participants. That was the zero line, so to speak, and in the wargame, we found a way to estimate the behaviour and action of the market participants in the market observed. Such a scenario, in which one assumes that everything only changes to the same extent as it has changed so far, is also called the trend scenario.

But what if the market will change due to external influences? Vinyl disc players, stagecoaches, typewriters and fax machines are good examples. Offering these products is no longer a viable line of business because their markets have changed due to external factors. The following process will be about assessing such conceivable changes for the future. The fact that I do not go into the actions of competitors has only something to do with the complexity of the considerations: If, for example, you wanted to run through four external factors with three characteristics (weakens, remains the same, strengthens), you would already theoretically have $3^4 = 81$ scenarios. Each minimal action of a market participant (*does nothing* or *changes something*) at least doubles these options. With three competitors we are then already at 648 scenarios … well, and so on. That was the event funnel we were talking about. Remember it?

In the workshops we conduct, we, therefore, try to arrive at around three to a maximum of five initial sets for developing future scenarios, disregarding the reactions of market participants. In practice, it has proven successful to incorporate these into the developed future scenarios only during real planning. If, for example, VW has identified the reactions of Opel and Nissan and their driving factors in the wargame, it is also easy to thread them onto the future scenario "There are no more cars with internal combustion engines" or "The main use is car-sharing services".

Furthermore, quite pragmatically: A workshop has to be fun if it is to be successful. Varied workshops can last up to a maximum of 3 days—after that, they become boring and exhausting. So let's postpone the fine planning of the scenarios until afterward and into the strategists' area of responsibility …

Take all the influencing factors worked out by the participants and think about how these factors could change. These are the "characteristics". If you now combine the influencing factors in the respective characteristics in a meaningful way, you have created a set of assumptions as a starting point for your scenario game. Let's take a closer look at how something like this could look in concrete terms using the example of the automotive market.

Now start selecting the "most important" sets of reasonable assumptions together with the participants, but no more than the number of teams you can form. Assign one team at a time to work on one set. The task is:

Let the teams work freely and openly on these topics. If the energy is still there, even slide in an iteration by having the teams briefly present interim results and give each other feedback and suggestions.

Task

What will change for us and our business model if you adopt the following changes:

"Here comes the set for this group to work on.

Please develop these assumptions five years into the future. Proceed strictly logically, but do not limit yourself by considering probabilities. You should also consider improbable results as long as they can be derived strictly logically from these assumptions.

Consider also indirect derivations: For example, a radical shortage of oil, even if only temporarily, could promote other developments that have an impact on the "motor vehicle manufacturing" business model because the need to develop alternative transport options increases dramatically.

After this exercise, have the final scenarios presented and summarize the findings. As a result, you end up with a set of scenarios that relate to your business area and business model and that show you the mentioned framework in which the future relevant to your business could move.

If all went well, you could now have at the end of the workshop:

- An assessment of how your current strategy is likely to be viewed and responded to by other market participants and competitors—you may also have creative approaches to adapting your original strategic plan if this has proved necessary;

- but especially a mostly very plausible result of the reaction test;
- Initial ideas on possible scenarios for how your market could develop in the future;
- A highly motivated team to work on these issues;
- Possibly even a few more cool ideas from Google Day.

Even though I use the subjunctive when describing results for good reasons—not every workshop is equally successful—I have achieved good results in the past with such workshops, whose predictions were accurate for many years, especially concerning the reactions of competitors.

So: What a successful workshop! You are now very well equipped to plan the future of your company. Because that's what you don't have yet: a concrete, manageable plan with timings, responsibilities and budgets behind it. This step—to turn a great raw material into the finished cake—is the task of the employees to whom you want to put or have already put the strategic planning in their hands. The workshop was the kick-off for laying the foundation—a kind of creative catalyst that must now be followed by hard planning work. No—even if I may have given this impression at the beginning—you don't get the future for free!

And one final note about the workshop: So do you now hold the perfect blueprint for building your future management workshop? No, by no means! If you take a closer look, you'll quickly conclude that some of what I've described here doesn't fit for you and that you want to change it. Go for it! I don't think I've ever run two workshops that were the same. So why should you start with that?

Important Questions and Tips for the Future Workshop

1. **Do you need to schedule a Google Day?**
   Not necessarily. But if creative work is not one of the main activities in your company, then this is most certainly a sensible start.
2. **Is the wargame required to the extent described?**
   If I had to design the workshop for the search engine division at Google (forgive my grand ambitions!), I'm sure it would look different because there simply aren't any real competitors to walk in their shoes. But the wargame is fun when teams start competing "against each other". And with that, something like this is definitely a good tool for the workshop.
3. **Do you have to plan for future scenarios to be this short or this long?**
   Of course, this also depends on your task. The shorter the time frame for which you want to plan your strategy or review an already planned strategy, the less worthwhile future scenarios are. Wargames that are extended in time may then yield better results.

4. **Is it worth taking a quantitative approach to future scenarios?**
   Yes, with the restrictions already mentioned. But in no case—as already described—should you try to do this as part of the workshop. But there is nothing against letting your strategy team think in numbers in the subsequent process as well. But: stop them when they start getting pseudo-scientifically precise. A number that cannot be logically justified has no place in your scenario!

You see: You have the free choice. Use it!

8 Never Again: Creative Crisis Management for the Time after Corona

Abstract

Crisis management mostly is understood either as a communication issue or as an action plan in the event of a crisis. In this chapter, I present the third variant: You can creatively prepare for potential crises with the help of the tools already presented because crises—even completely unexpected pandemics—are nothing more than a special form of the future for which you can prepare with good future scenarios.

Those who prepare their own company's future with the help of the techniques described so far already have all the tools in hand to professionalize crisis management with manageable effort. This is less about the usual aspects of crisis management such as crisis communication, quality management, or crisis prevention. Instead, I will describe a holistic concept with which you can prepare for crises and also counter them in an emergency. The special thing about this is that you can directly apply all the principles you have worked out so far, especially the ten steps of successful future management.

In the first edition of this book, I pointed out how similar good crisis management and future management are. But Corona has changed everything, including this book—and especially this chapter. Those who, as corporate managers, still believe that one does not need to prepare for crises have learned unfortunately nothing from Corona! Could the governments of the world have kept hospital beds and protective clothing on hand? Of course, they could! Could business leaders have asked themselves how to survive the total failure of a company for a month or two? Of course! But in both cases, thinking about this is unpleasant and sometimes painful: What is the cost of excellent hospitals and stored surpluses of medicines,

H. Hilbig, *Shaping the Future of Your Business*,
https://doi.org/10.1007/978-3-658-35349-0_8

equipment and protective clothing that will almost certainly (!) never be used? What is the cost of leaving profits in the company as an equity ratio instead of ensuring maximum profit for shareholders? How much do you pay for supply chains that don't rely on the cheapest supplier? Supply chains whose success is based on tiny in-house warehouses and just-in-time deliveries from their suppliers … The problem with such "wasted investments" insecurity is that, with the benefit of hindsight, any know-it-all critic can declare that this money has been spent completely uselessly and is therefore lost. While crisis managers who act well are admired with awe, politicians and managers are denied the medals for good precautions, as the consequence of good precautions is that nothing happens!

Politicians, entrepreneurs, CEOs, and shareholders will have to learn to face up to these trade-offs and take probabilities into account—even if they are quite improbable. Corona has shown that a probability, however low, is not "zero". But to make those trade-offs, you need scenarios of what could theoretically happen. Yes, that's right—scenarios like the ones you learned about in this book for preparing for the future!

▶ **Attention**

Under the title "Crisis Management "there is a large amount of management literature that deals in very different ways with the question of how to deal with crises. If you look closely, however, many of the works only deal with partial aspects of the topic, such as *crisis communication, crisis prevention* or *quality management.* However, anyone who has ever experienced a real corporate crisis and possibly had to master it themselves knows that it is not enough to pay attention to such partial aspects.

Excellent crisis management can be identified by

- The crisis is identified as early as possible.
- Many areas are well prepared and quickly pulling in the same direction.
- Communication, defensive measures and solutions are developed in parallel and implemented in a coordinated manner.

The exciting thing now is that it is possible to prepare for the emergence of a crisis in the same way that we have discussed future scenarios up to this point because

- A crisis is per se an unexpected, future event, which can be
- in retrospect, can always be derived as a logical consequence of one's economic actions, and

- for which one can prepare oneself as far as possible via a series of well-planned scenarios.

The unexpected—logical consequence of actions—scenarios: If that doesn't sound familiar! And so all the mechanisms for planning for the future discussed so far can also be applied analogously to crisis management. Let us briefly review the characteristics for successful future management from Sect. 3.4 and see how they can be adapted to crises.

8.1 Resilience: Remaining Ready for Change

One of the most important qualities in crisis management is to be open to potential crises. Hardly any assertion is heard more often at meetings, congresses or trade shows than: "It won't affect us. Nothing has ever happened to us before." Or even: "We don't need much preparation. If a crisis comes, I (we) can decide very quickly what to do."

Talk to those colleagues who have already been through a real crisis and ask them if they agree with these two theses. That's the moment when I like to ask those skeptics if they would fasten their seatbelts on an airplane, and if so, why. Isn't it enough to buckle up when you hit turbulence?

Have you moved away from such positions since the virus took hold of us all?

Crises are admittedly rare and thus unlikely—pandemics even rarer—but when they do occur, they come with enormous consequential damage. How big was your loss in fiscal 2020? So the next time you fasten your seatbelt on an airplane, take a minute to think about whether you shouldn't also protect your company with a crisis management concept.

8.2 Thinking about Processes

When a crisis is already around the corner, you have little time to worry about planned procedures. This already starts with an alarming chain that should work even in the middle of the night on December 25. Exactly on such a day in 2004, one of the biggest disasters for the people in Asia began with the seaquake Those were the days when we all learned the word *tsunami*…

One of the best-prepared companies was TUI, which had already put together an international crisis management team on December 26, and was able to help the affected passengers most quickly and effectively thanks to predefined procedures.

Crises are by no means all the same, but they can usually be handled according to certain schemes. However, you need to have these processes in place, just as you do in future management if you don't want to be surprised by a crisis in your nightgown. Just ask yourself whether your company could ever round up a group of decision-makers unexpectedly and unannounced in the early morning of December 26 (!).

8.3 Raising Employee Awareness

As with the future issue, you are also dependent on the early detection of possible crises, so that you can perceive the early warning signals that announce a crisis. Are your employees on board? If they know about crisis management and if you have set up an alarm chain that is accessible and known to everyone, then your prepared processes can take effect. Imagine, however, that your receptionist doesn't know what to do with 20 police officers waving a search warrant at 6:00 a.m. and setting off to dismantle your central company server without much questioning. To secure evidence and with a search warrant in hand, police officers usually do not ask long, if you could kindly provide a complete data copy.

8.4 Working Holistically: Crisis Are Not a Departmental Issue

When identifying as well as combating a crisis, it is necessary to draw on expertise from all areas. For example, even if you are "only" expecting a product crisis, for which you need the expertise and creativity of product management, you need to talk to your investors, your customers and the press, sending the right, credible and trustworthy message to your banks and other stakeholders. And to be able to identify possible crisis scenarios, you also need experts from all functional areas!

8.5 Developing Scenarios

Nothing makes the similarity of the two fields in their approach clearer than this point. Whereas in future management you have to look for possible developments due to external influences and think them through to then be able to define a strategy for action, crisis management uses the same methodology to consider both internal and external factors that could lead to crises and then play through these cases in the scenario technique.

As with the preparation for future markets, you have to find a selection of typical representatives of all conceivable crises for which you develop suitable countermeasures during the strategy development. As serious as this topic is—working out such scenarios can be quite fun, as the participants have to come up with really bizarre cases.

8.6 Paying Attention to Small Deviations

If big changes in the area of future management are announced by small things that you only have to notice, then this is even more true for crisis management. The early warning management that you need for your strategic planning can also be mobilized identically for the early detection of crises!

8.7 Paying Attention to Marginal Issues

Crises often arise out of issues that you do not pay the most attention to in everyday life. This is completely logical because, with the topics you have in focus, you perceive every change immediately and react accordingly. On the other hand, you can't pay attention to everything—no company has such resources.

So what can be done? The most sensible option is to identify potential trouble spots beforehand and play through reactions to them (see Sect. 7.1 Developing scenarios) and then regularly sensitise the conceivable contact points of a crisis to them (see Sect. 6.6 Raising employee awareness).

8.8 Examine Yourself

The "Make yourself competitive" step naturally involves (regularly) checking to see where there might be weaknesses in your business model and then addressing them yourself before a competitor does. For crisis management, you go through the same process of checking—and, if you identify weaknesses, act yourself before the crisis is triggered.

For both topics—future and crisis management—do not underestimate this step: Just because an option is unlikely, it can still occur and cause incredible damage. Although the chance of winning the lottery is significantly smaller than the probability of your company being raided by the public prosecutor's office, 29 million German people play the lottery (Institut für Demoskopie Allensbach 2017). And the most surprising thing is: some of them win millions every week! Although the likelihood of a pandemic, which could lead to an economic standstill worldwide, was extraordinarily unlikely … well, you know where this is going.

8.9 Remain Vigilant

As the future changes, so do crisis risk. Things you could do unhindered just 10 years ago can now—thanks to the omnipresence of social media—trigger a devastating shitstorm. Up until 30 years ago, you could find complete resident data in book form in every phone booth, and companies and government agencies were collecting, linking, and analyzing it back then. Today, companies feel like their backs are up against the wall every time a few hundred customer data are hacked somewhere.

Sometimes such changes in the expectations of customers and other stakeholders come with a roar—but often they come rather creepily. So quietly, that it has not yet been noticed within the company. The diesel scandal is a good example of this. A small piece of software that changes the measured values just a tiny bit, to the extent that it is just passing the authorities' emissions test. A tiny bit of cheating! Unfortunately, the perception of people and authorities worldwide concerning car emissions had changed from "it's not so bad" to "we're serious about the climate"—and a little cheating turned into a crisis that endangered the company, which, in addition to monetary values, also lost an incredible amount of trust.

Introducing holistic, preventive crisis management correctly in a company is of course a topic with which one could fill a book of its own. With this short excursion into the topic, I would just like to invite you to invest the tools that you practice in the future for your future management in this part of the future provision.

The inventor of the airbag for children in cars will probably never get as much applause as someone who rescues a single baby from a crashed car—although he has probably saved the lives of thousands of children. So even though preventing a crisis from happening in the first place is far less spectacular than actively managing a crisis—with good crisis management, consisting of prevention, early detection, and scenario-based crisis management, you save your company more money than your marketing can spend with just one crisis prevented.

Reference

Institut für Demoskopie Allensbach (2017) Allensbacher Markt- und Werbeträgeranalyse. https://www.ifd-allensbach.de/fileadmin/AWA/AWA2017/Codebuchausschnitte/AWA2017_Codebuch_Sport.pdf. Zugegriffen: 22. Mai 2020

9 Background Information

Abstract

Anyone who talks about future strategies and necessary future management—even in internal meetings—needs good arguments because the future can be discussed creatively in a risk-free manner—as it's not yet there! In addition to hopefully many thought-provoking ideas, which you will find in this book, you also need confidence in your argumentation and—sometimes—a quick response. In this chapter you will therefore find quotations, sources for the case studies, and book recommendations on the most important aspects of planning for the future.

9.1 Quotes from People Who Seemed to Know better

I don't know about you: Some of the quotes make me think. Sometimes because of the wisdom contained in such words, sometimes because of the—in retrospect—obvious error. In this book, I have deliberately tried to point out at every opportunity that the path to the future of a company must begin in the way, its leaders think. Those who are certain that they can assess everything correctly will be hit all the harder by chance. Now, however, it seems to be one of the particularly preferred management traits to have to exude such certainty. To question oneself, one's experience and one's knowledge again and again is (still) rather frowned upon.

Perhaps this little collection of useful quotes of great and less great people will help a little to awaken such meaningful self-doubt. So use them often on your way to preparing your company for such a future process!

H. Hilbig, *Shaping the Future of Your Business*,
https://doi.org/10.1007/978-3-658-35349-0_9

Oh yes, in case you are missing the quotes of the present here: These are the forecasts, which we still seriously discuss today—and about which our grandchildren will then laugh heartily!

- **1876—An early internal Western Union paper on the idea of a "telephone":** "This 'telephone' has too many shortcomings to be seriously considered as a means of communications. The device is inherently of no value for us."
- **1896—Sir William Preece, Chief Engineer of the British Post Office to Graham Bell, when the latter had demonstrated to him the practicality of the telephone:** "No, Sir. The Americans may need the telephone, but we do not. We have a great many couriers."
- **1897—William Thomson (Lord Kelvin), President of the Royal Society:** "Radio has no future."
- **1899—C. H. Duell, Commissioner of the United States Patent Office:** "Everything that can be invented has been invented."
- **1902—German emperor Wilhelm II:** "I believe in the horse; the automobile is a passing phenomenon."
- **1911—Ferdinant Foch, marshal in the French army and professor of military tactics:** "Aeroplanes are an interesting gimmick, but of no military use."
- **1927—Harry M. Warner, Warner Brothers:** "Who wants to hear actors talk?"
- **1943—Thomas Watson, president of IBM:** "I think there is a world market for maybe five computers."
- **1949—Computer expert John von Neumann, US scientist and one of the fathers of modern computer science:** "It would appear that we have already reached the limits of what is possible to achieve with computer technology, although one should be careful with such statements, as they tend to sound pretty silly in 5 years."
- **1962—Decca Records (when they rejected The Beatles):** "We don't like their sounds. Groups of guitars are on the way out."
- **1977—Kenneth Olsen, president Digital Equipment Corp:** "There is no reason for anyone to want a computer at home."
- **1989—Bill Gates, Microsoft:** "We will never make a 32-bit operating system."
- **1991—Brad Silverberg, Microsoft:** "DOS will be with us forever. We've learned how passionate people are about DOS."
- **1993—Bill Gates, Microsoft:** "Internet? It's just hype."
- **2005—Sir Alan Sugar, founder of electronics company Amstrad:** "Next Christmas the iPod will be dead, finished, gone, broken."

- **2007—Steve Balmer (Microsoft CEO):** "There's no chance that the iPhone is going to get any significant market share. No chance."
- **2015—Matthias Müller, then CEO of Porsche AG (later CEO of VW AG):** "For me, autonomous driving represents hype that cannot be justified by anything."
- **2016—Matthias Horx (founder of the Zukunftsinstitut) on autonomous driving**: "Only when we can turn the driver's seat around and work, read or make love in the car completely undisturbed, will a new car age really emerge. That won't be the case before 20 years ..." **9.2 For reference: Links and sources of the case studies**

I can hardly warn you, not to use examples lightly and without intensive research for your future planning, if I don't share my sources with you for your onw reference. Not everything I was able to research has found space in the preceding pages. However, much of what has been omitted may well have relevance to your planning. Therefore, here is an almost complete list of the sources that can be read.

Changing the Brand Essence (Apple)

Company:	Apple Inc
	www.Apple.com
Acting persons:	Steve jobs, CEO
Strategic approach:	Apple has created innovation itself. In the process: Constantly questioning themselves as well as also making radical decisions with regard to the product range.
Sources:	For apple, too, there are of course a vast number of sources that can easily be found by doing a simple search on the web. Therefore, only three examples of sources are mentioned here. The history of the company, which is largely based on products, can be read well here (among many other sources): http://www.mac-history.de/zeitleiste-die-entwicklung-von-apple-seit-1976 More background information on decisions made in the course of product development can be found in the authorised biography of Steve jobs by Walter Isaacson (publisher: C. Bertelsmann Verlag; 2011). The long-term turnover and profit figures of Apple as well as the economic importance of the individual product groups—and thus the consequences of various decisions made by jobs—can be understood very well here: https://www.macprime.ch/wissen/article/apple-geschaeftszahlen-analysen-grafiken-umsatz-gewinn-verkaufszahlen

Change of Concept of a Brand (Casio G-Shock)

Company:	Casio Computer Co Ltd., Japan
	www.Casio.com
Acting persons:	Kazuo Kashio, president and chairman Kikuo Ibe, Watch designer
Strategic approach:	Close to the market, quickly recognising new product trends and reacting boldly.
Sources:	The story of the G-Shock is largely aptly told here: https://www.g-central.com/g-shock-history/ On the idea and development of the watch, designer Ibe gives an interview here: https://www.youtube.com/watch?v=pqHy3h9IsaE The history of the company itself is presented quite clearly here: https://www.watchonista.com/articles/history/history-quartz-weekend-part-3-casio-digital-revolution The variety of products that Casio has developed over the decades can be understood quite well here: https://world.casio.com/corporate/history/chronology/ All other details of the history come from personal experience: I was head of marketing at Casio between 1985 and 1995.

Digitization (Eastman Kodak)

Company:	Eastman Kodak Ltd
	www.Kodak.com
Acting persons:	Steven session
Strategic approach:	Using one's own market position to stabilise the market
Sources:	There are many sources on Kodak, so I will only give one example here: How Kodak failed Forbes, January 2013 www.forbes.com/sites/chunkamui/2012/01/18/how-kodak-failed/3/#14966544a97PersönlichkeitsprofilInsightsdiscovery The story of the digital camera was told by the inventor Steven Sasson himself in many interviews: The man who invented the future Spiegel Online, October 2015 http://www.spiegel.de/einestages/digitalkamera-erfinder-steve-sasson-ueber-kodaks-pleite-a-1057653.html David LaChapelle talks with the inventor of the digital Camera about the death of film photography Papermag.com, May 2015 http://www.papermag.com/david-lachapelle-talks-with-the-inventor-of-the-digital-camera-about-t-1439209397.html Life lecture by Steven Sasson at Linda Hall Library, 2011: https://vimeo.com/31404047

Innovation Management for Typewriters (Olympia)

Company:	Olympia Büromaschinenwerke AG AEG, DaimlerBenz
	Keine Onlinepräsenz (firma existiert nicht mehr)
Acting persons:	Miscellaneous
Strategic approach:	Market seen as evolutionary and stable
Sources:	Olympia's decline was also a long-term process with many factors. I have gathered details from background discussions with former Olympia employees. The following pages provide a good overview: Fear of the holiday Zeit Online, May 1992 http://www.zeit.de/1992/21/angst-vor-dem-urlaub/komplettansicht The chronicle of Olympia Werke AG, leer plant Journal of the former Olympia employees, September 2007 http://beispiele.elkat.de/olympia/aktuell/pdf/10009.pdf Into bankruptcy instead of the future Nwzonline.de, May 2011 https://www.nwzonline.de/wirtschaft/weser-ems/in-die-pleite-statt-in-die-zukunft_a_1.0.610.885597.html The history of the Olympia-Werke itself is described as authentically as possible in the current article at Wikipedia: https://de.wikipedia.org/wiki/Olympia-Werke

Change in Product Orientation (Rügenwalder Mühle)

Company:	Rügenwalder Mühle Carl Müller GmbH und Co. KG
	https://www.ruegenwalder.de/
Acting persons:	Christian Rauffus, owner and CEO Bodo Göben, CEO, head of production and marketing
Strategic approach:	Competing with yourself before the market does
Sources:	A lot of the details about Rügenwalder Mühle's strategic move come from a personal interview with CEO Godo Röben in June 2017. Also: It's all about the meatless sausage Handelsblatt, August 2016 http://www.handelsblatt.com/my/unternehmen/handel-konsumgueter/ruegenwalder-muehle-meica-herta-es-geht-um-die-fleischlose-wurst/14448496.html?ticket=ST-605477-JdhlPvTs3KXNnzwKugeD-ap4 A sausage manufacturer wants to get away from meat FAZ, November 2016 http://www.faz.net/aktuell/wirtschaft/unternehmen/ruegenwalder-muehle-will-trend-zur-vegetarischen-wurst-ausbauen-14527466.html Lucky Zeit Online, May 2015 http://www.zeit.de/2015/19/ruegenwalder-muehle-vegetarische-wurst The sausage is the cigarette of the future Spiegel Online, April 2015 http://www.spiegel.de/wirtschaft/ruegenwalder-muehle-verkauft-vegetarische-wurst-a-1023898.html

Perfect Fit (Ikea)

Company:	Ikea
	http://www.ikea.com
Acting persons:	Ingvar Kamprad, owner und CEO
Strategic approach:	Perfect adaptation to every market change
Sources:	Probably the most online information on the history of Ikea's rise comes from Ikea itself. The most detailed version is probably on Wikipedia: https://de.wikipedia.org/wiki/IKEA A light version is even available as an animated video on YouTube: https://www.youtube.com/watch?v=e-kfzCcYruU A clear distinction must be made between the early years (which are the subject of the chapter in this book) and the later years of the company. There are quite critical articles about the latter in particular: Rich, poor man Spiegel Online, March 2006 http://www.spiegel.de/wirtschaft/ikea-gruender-kamprad-wird-80-reicher-armer-mann-a-408621.html The unvarnished truth about the Ikea founder Welt Online, November 2009 https://www.welt.de/wirtschaft/article5345916/Die-ungeschminkte-Wahrheit-ueber-den-Ikea-Gruender.html

Further Reading

Naturally, there is an almost unbelievable selection of background literature on the topics addressed in this book. The following very small list should therefore rather be understood as a reading suggestion if you want to dive deeper into this topic

On the Unpredictability of the Future

Brater J (2012) Keine Ahnung, aber davon viel–die peinlichsten Prognosen der Welt. Ullstein, Berlin

Ebert V (2016) Unberechenbar–warum das Leben zu komplex ist um es perfekt zu planen. Rowohlt Polaris, Reinbek

Silver N (2012) The signal and the noise: why so many predictions fail-but some Don't. Penguin Press, New York

Ideas and Forecasts for the Future

Gassmann et al (2018) Smart City–Innovationen für die vernetzte Stadt. Hanser, München
Hermann A, Brenner W (2018) Die autonome Revolution–wie selbstfahrende Autos unsere Straßen erobern. Fazit Communication, Frankfurt a. M
Harari YN (2016) Homo Deus–A Brief History of Tomorrow. Penguin Books, New York, Vintage

Beck, München

Herger M (2018) The last Driver's license holder has already been born. McGraw-Hill Education, New York
Keese C (2017) Silicon Germany–Wie wir die digitale Transformation schaffen. Knaus, München
Levine R et al (2000) The Cluetrain manifesto. Econ, Berlin
Yogeshwar R (2017) Nächste Ausfahrt Zukunft. Kiepenheuer & Wisch, Köln
Walsh T (2017) It's alive! Artificial intelligence from the logic piano to killer robots. University Press & Black, Melbourne
Walker M (2015) Germany 2064. Diogenes, Zürich

Studies on the (Mis) Success Secrets of Successful Companies

Barabba VP (2011) The decision loom. Triarchy Press, Devon UK
Barabba VP, Zaltmann G (1991) Hearing the voice of the market. Harvard Business School Press & Ueberreuter, Wien
Carroll PB, Mui C (2009) Billion dollar lessons. Pengiun Group, New York
Collins J (2001) Good to great: why some companies make the leap… and others Don't. Random House Business, New York
Kirsh K (2012) How to kill your company. 50 ways your'e bleeding your organisation and damaging your caree. iUniverse, Bloomington

Thinking Errors and Pattern Recognition

Chang D-S (2016) Mein Hirn hat seinen eigenen Kopf: Wie wir andere und uns selbst wahrnehmen. Rowohlt Polaris, Reinbek
Dobelli R (2012) Die Kunst des klugen Handelns–52 Irrwege, die Sie besser anderen überlassen. Hanser, München
Dueck G (2015) Schwarmdumm–so blöd sind wir nur gemeinsam. Campus, Frankfurt a. M
Hilbig H (2015) Marketing sucht Zielgruppe oder Was macht der Gorilla am POS? Springer Gabler, Wiesbaden
Kahneman D (2011) Thinking, fast and slow. Macmillan Us, New york
Lindstrom M (2016) Small Data: Was Kunden wirklich wollen–wie man aus winzigen Hinweisen geniale Schlüsse zieht. Plassen, Kulmbach

Workshop and Organizational Concepts

Albers O (2001) Zukunftswerkstatt und Szenariotechnik: Schnell und innovativ die Unternehmenszukunft gestalten. Walhalla und Praetoria, Regensburg

Gilad B, Junginger MG (2010) Mit Business Wargaming den Markt erobern. Redline, München

Hirschmann W (2016) Gebrauchsanweisung für die Zukunft. Haufe Gruppe, Freiburg

Appendix A. Your Future: A Conclusion

Taking care of the future can be fun. Especially if you also enjoy technology. But desiring to shape the future is also hard work and requires courage. In my experience, the most important—and most difficult—step is the first one: As a company leader or division manager, you have to realize that you don't know your market or your industry. At least not in the future.

This sounds very esoteric, possibly even pathetic, but it is the basic prerequisite for future success. If you disagree, especially if you think you have your business under control, let me ask you a few questions.

Where do your experience and knowledge of your business come from?

It's from the past! Please try to realize this over and over again: Your experience has allowed you to succeed to this day. But success in the past is no guarantee for success in the future. And whether the methods you used to build your business and make it successful will still work in 2, 5 or 10 years, or whether your knowledge and experience will still have the same market value in 5 years, is at least questionable.

Your industry and your business are stable and not subject to fashionable fluctuations?

Sorry, but this is a fallacy. Whether you've been successful selling burgers, apps, or furniture: *Better* is always the enemy of *good*. Kodak was ninth in the world in the list of expensive companies, Olympia was the third largest manufacturer of office machines, and Nokia was the unbeatable leader in mobile phones—all of them operated in self-controlled, so-called "stable" markets ("people will always take pictures, write, and make phone calls"). And all three, despite all available resources and manpower, did not see the devastating impact coming. Among

H. Hilbig, *Shaping the Future of Your Business*,
https://doi.org/10.1007/978-3-658-35349-0

the last to move from stasis back to normal business after the 2021 viral crisis will be restaurants and airlines. How many of the major airlines and food chains will survive this crisis unscathed?

So are you sure that such a thing is not possible in your industry or all industries?

You have practiced the short decision-making paths that helped to positively master crises and changes in the past? Congratulations. Then you have done a lot right. In the past! I once strongly advised a company leader to look into setting up a crisis management system, as his business was highly susceptible to crises of confidence. However, the colleague could not be convinced, because he thought that in the event of a crisis he would only have to consult with his co-managing director—which, after all, would not be witchcraft. And with such short distances, one could react as quickly as possible. About 6 months after this conversation, a crisis came from a completely unexpected direction, which destroyed 80% of the global share value within a few days.

Your business is running so successfully that you can still deal with destructive forces when it's time?

This is certainly one of the more dangerous thoughts because it tempts people to want to keep the status quo. After a recent keynote, I had questions from an audience member who felt that the point about "competing with yourself" was counterproductive. After all, he said, as CEO his main task would be to increasing the well-being of the company, its employees, and its shareholders. If he were to give up existing business, he would be acting contrary to this mandate. My question in such cases is whether one has already dealt with the first part of the question—to first identify such ideas that could destroy one's business model. Only after you have identified such ideas, you can and must decide how to deal with them. By all means, deal with these ideas—if you don't, a (future) competitor will!

And then there is the not funny joke among mathematicians about how you as a passenger can best prevent a plane from being blown up by a bomb being taken on board? You take one on board yourself—because it is extremely unlikely—practically impossible—that two bombs are smuggled in on one plane. Mathematicians among themselves!

Any thought that a situation like the Corona pandemic could never happen again in the foreseeable future is an illusion! Already tomorrow a new, completely different virus could conquer the planet from somewhere. Therefore, my urgent advice:

▶ **Don't wait until the next unexpected event hits your business. Prepare yourself and your company—Now is the time.**

I wish you the best of luck with that!

Heino Hilbig.

Index

H. Hilbig, *Shaping the Future of Your Business*,
https://doi.org/10.1007/978-3-658-35349-0

The manufacturer's authorised representative in the EU is Springer Nature Customer Service Centre GmbH, Europaplatz 3, 69115 Heidelberg, Germany. If you have any concerns regarding our products, please contact ProductSafety@springernature.com

Printed and bound by CPI Group (UK) Ltd, Croydon, CR0 4YY
30/09/2026
02225707-0001